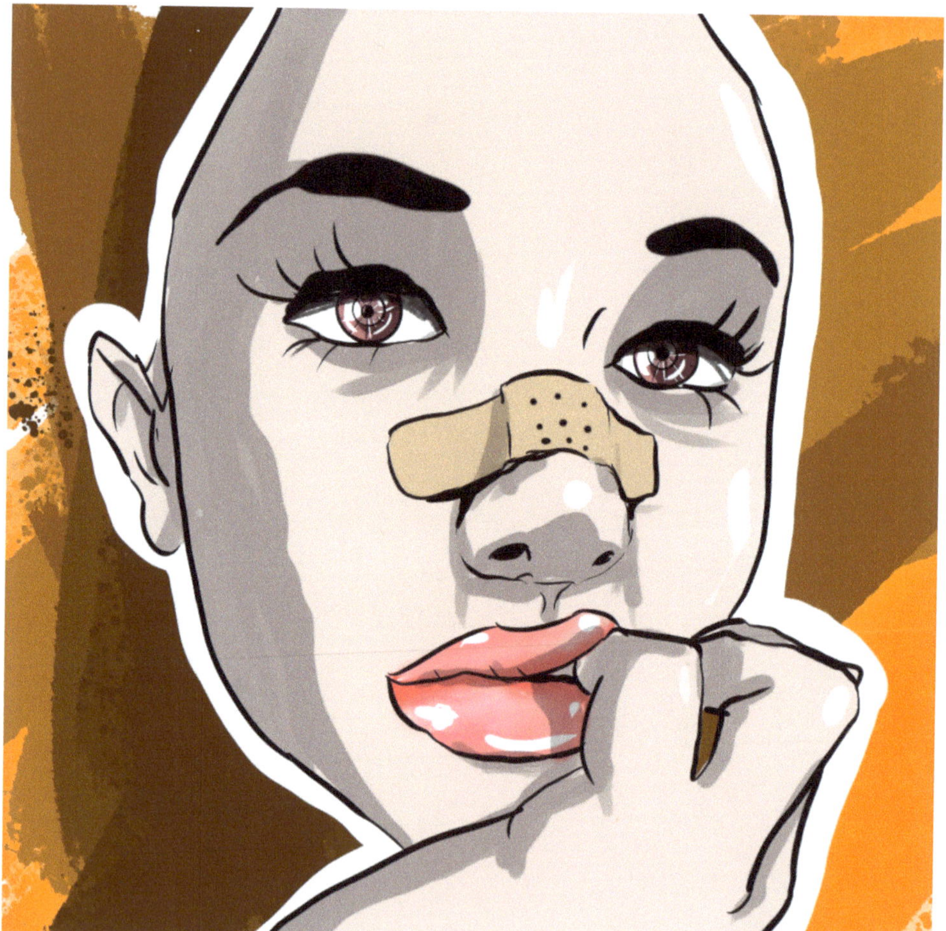

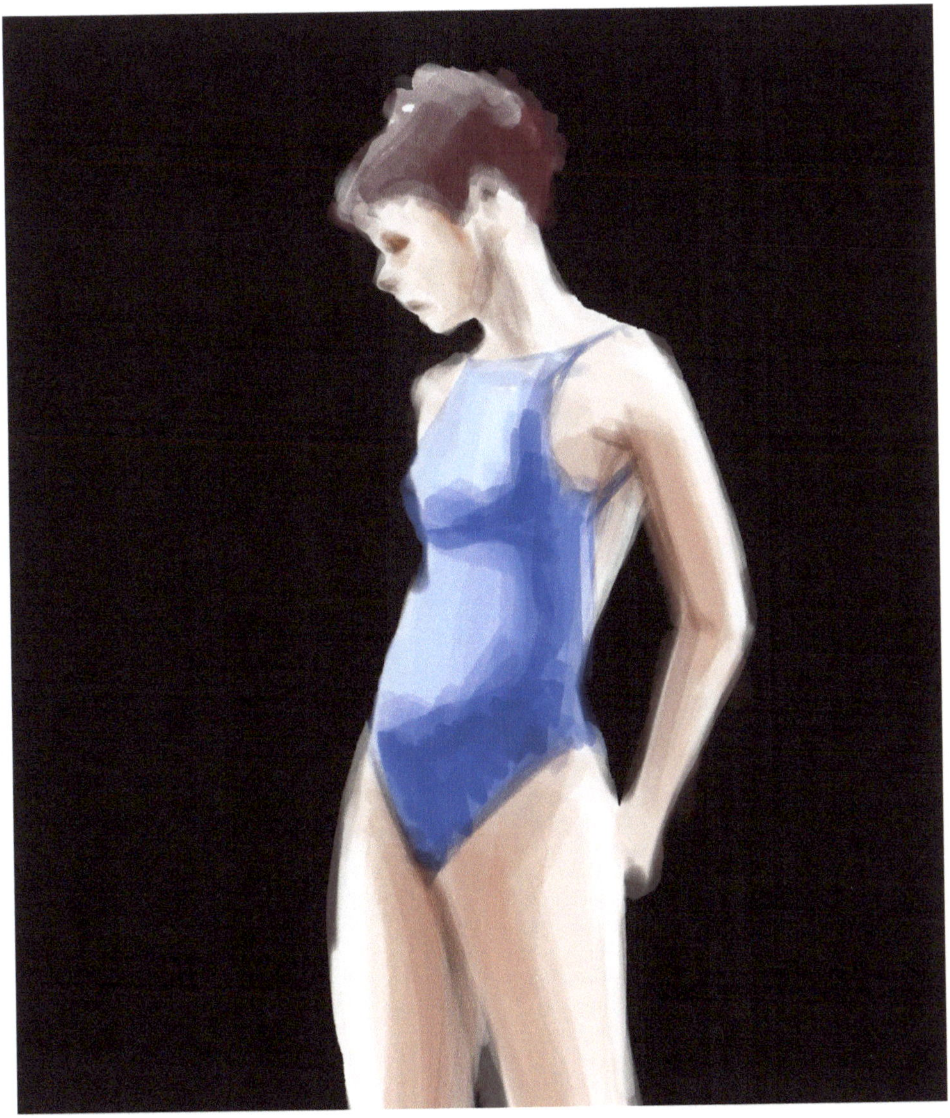

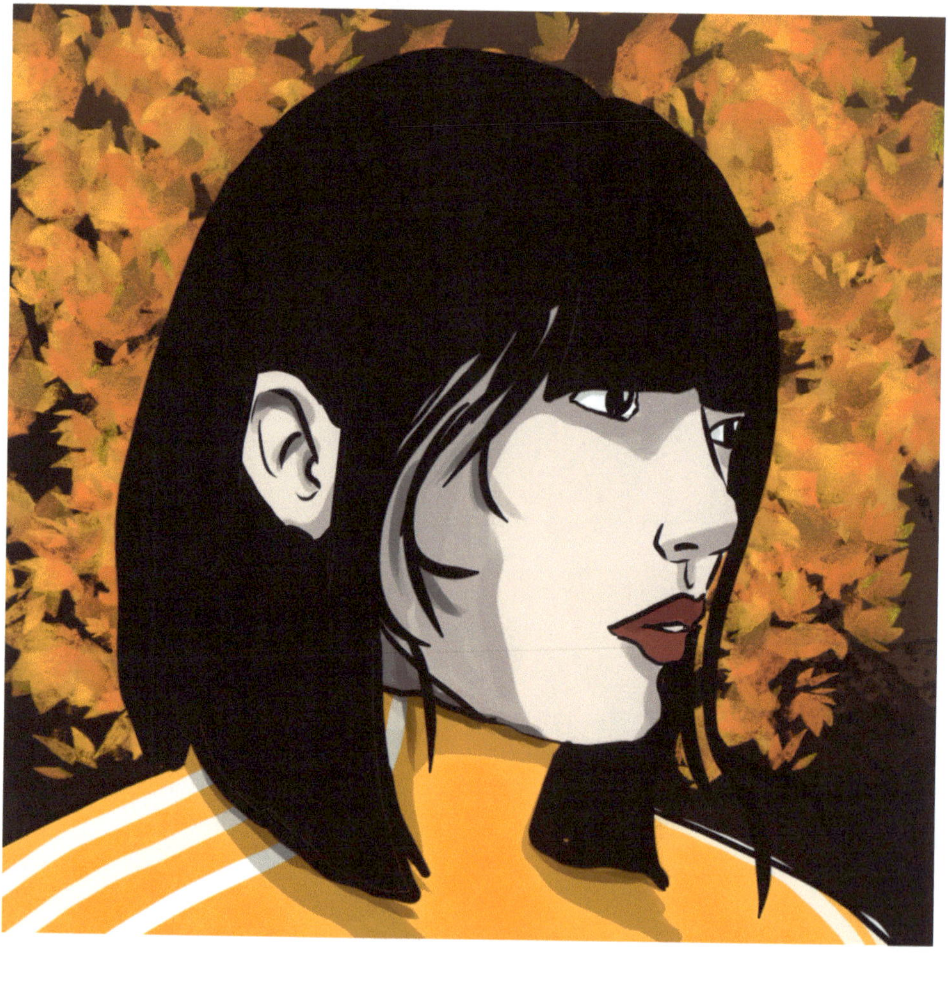

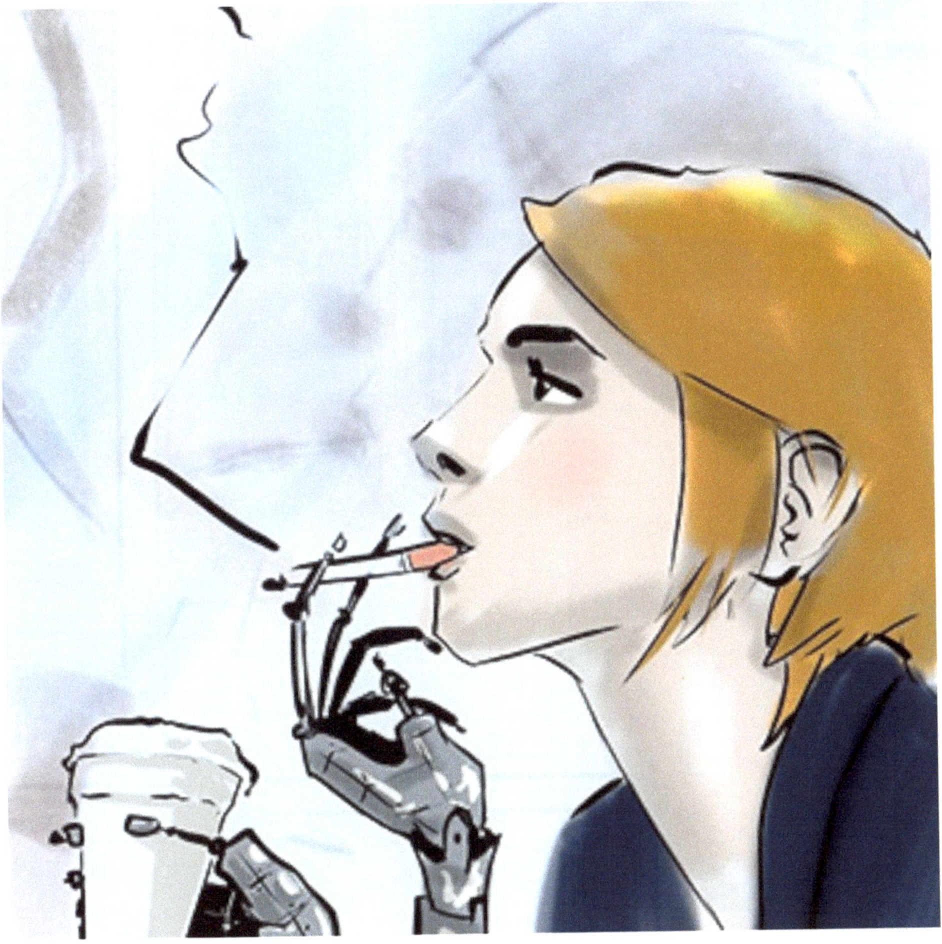

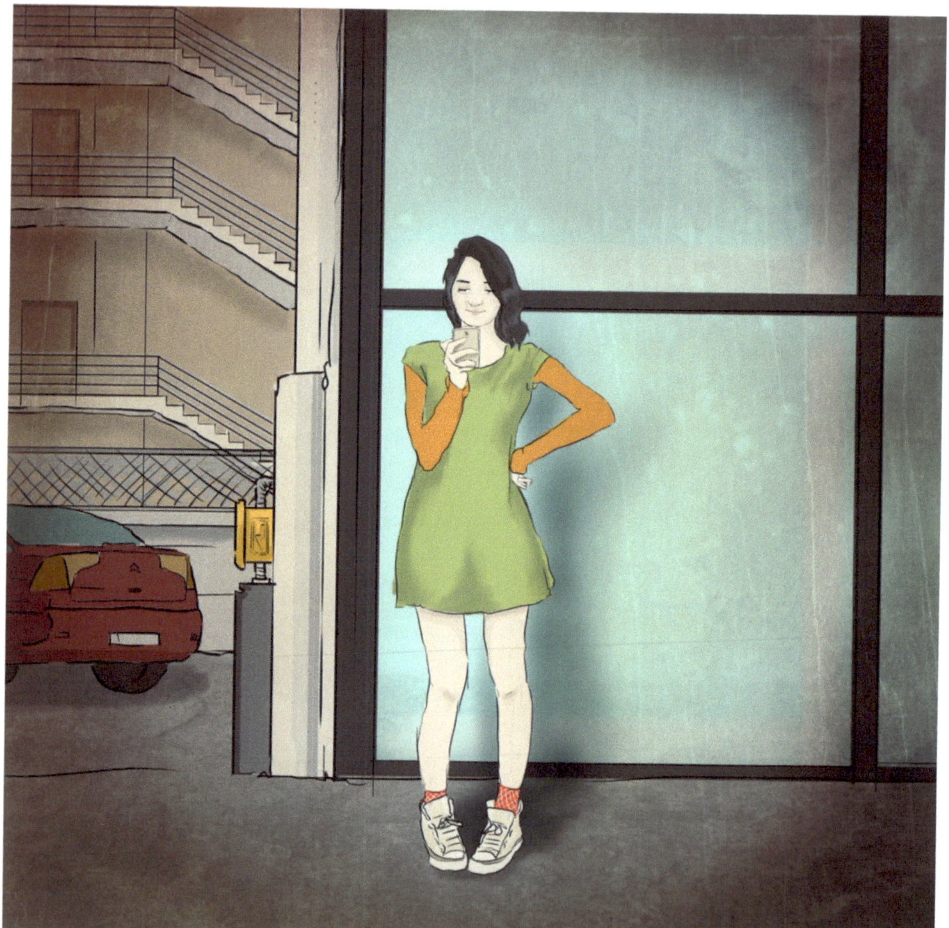

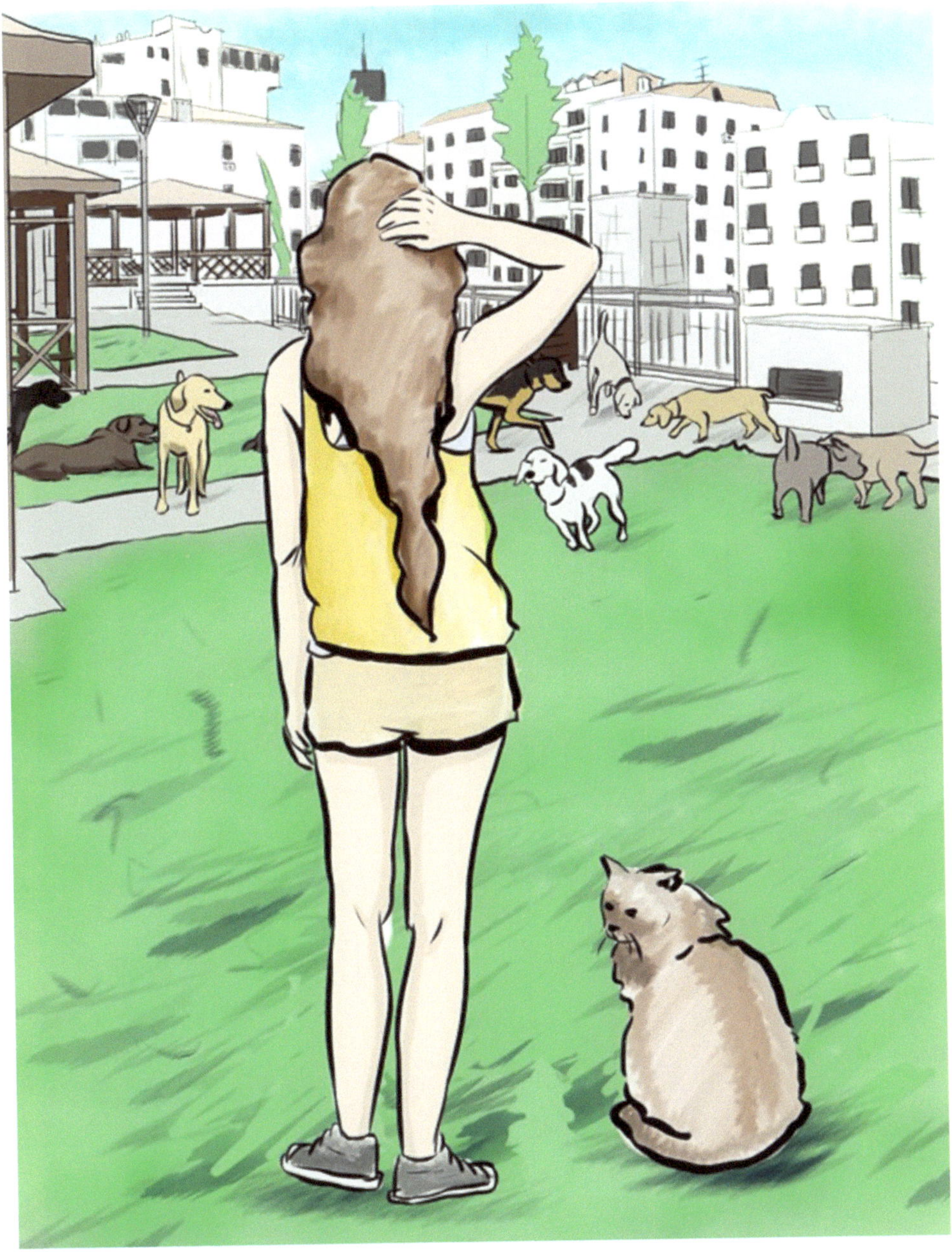

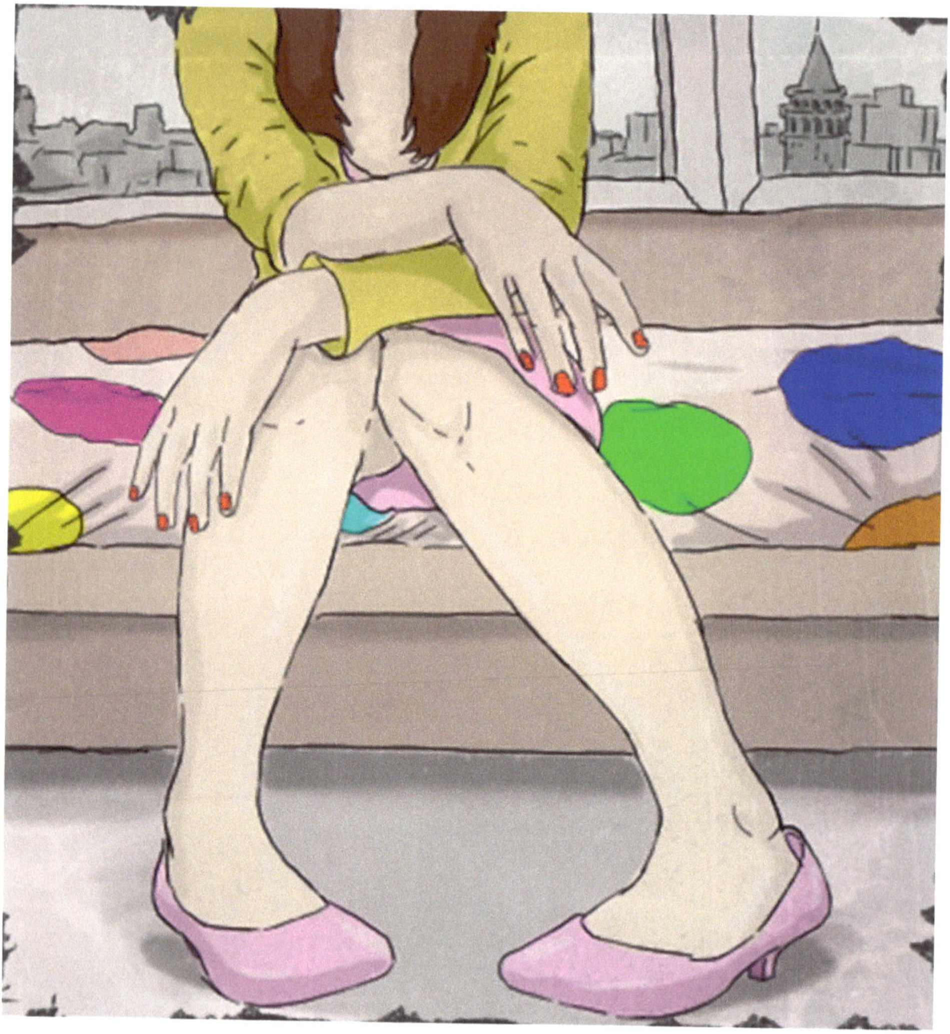

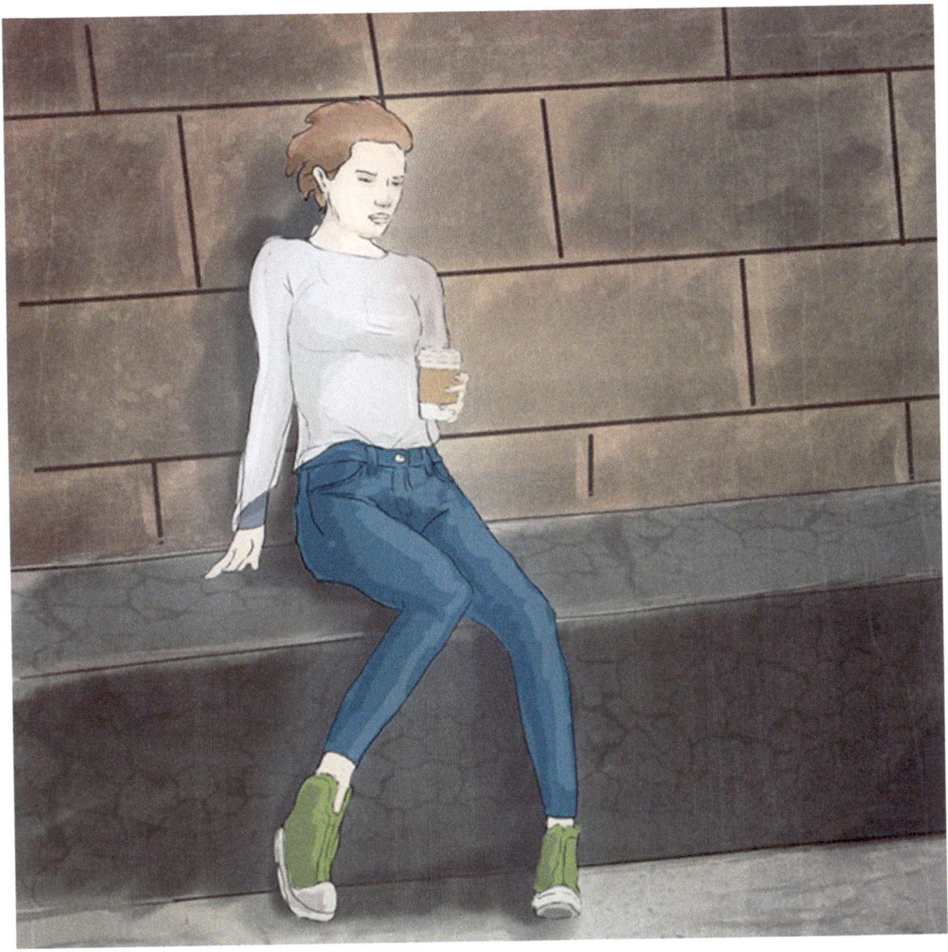

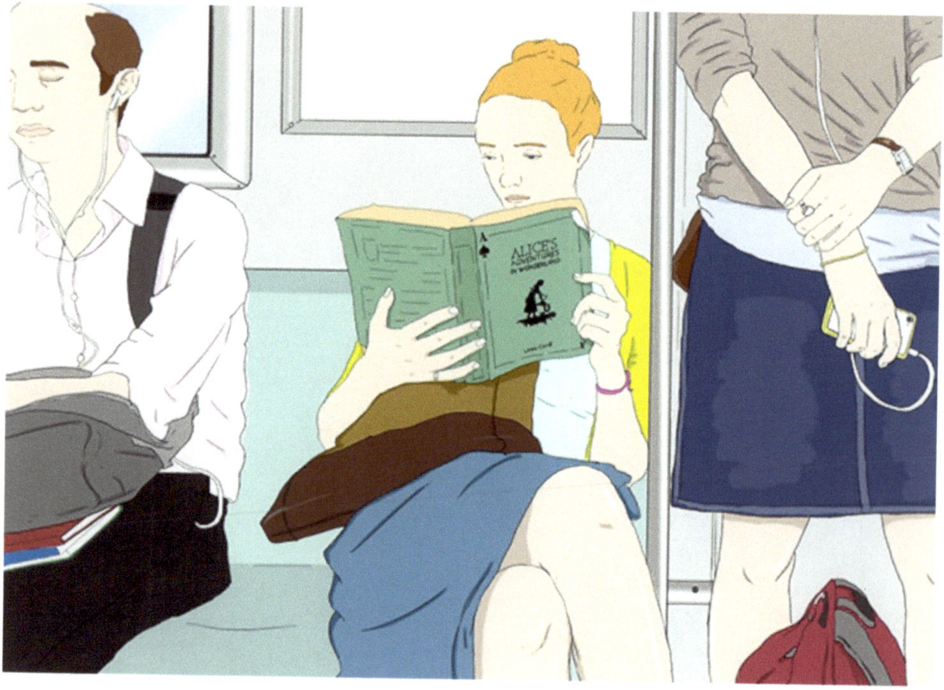
ALICE'S
ADVENTURES

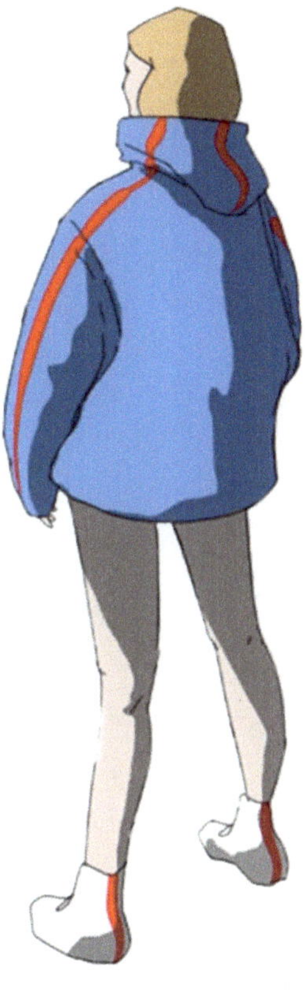

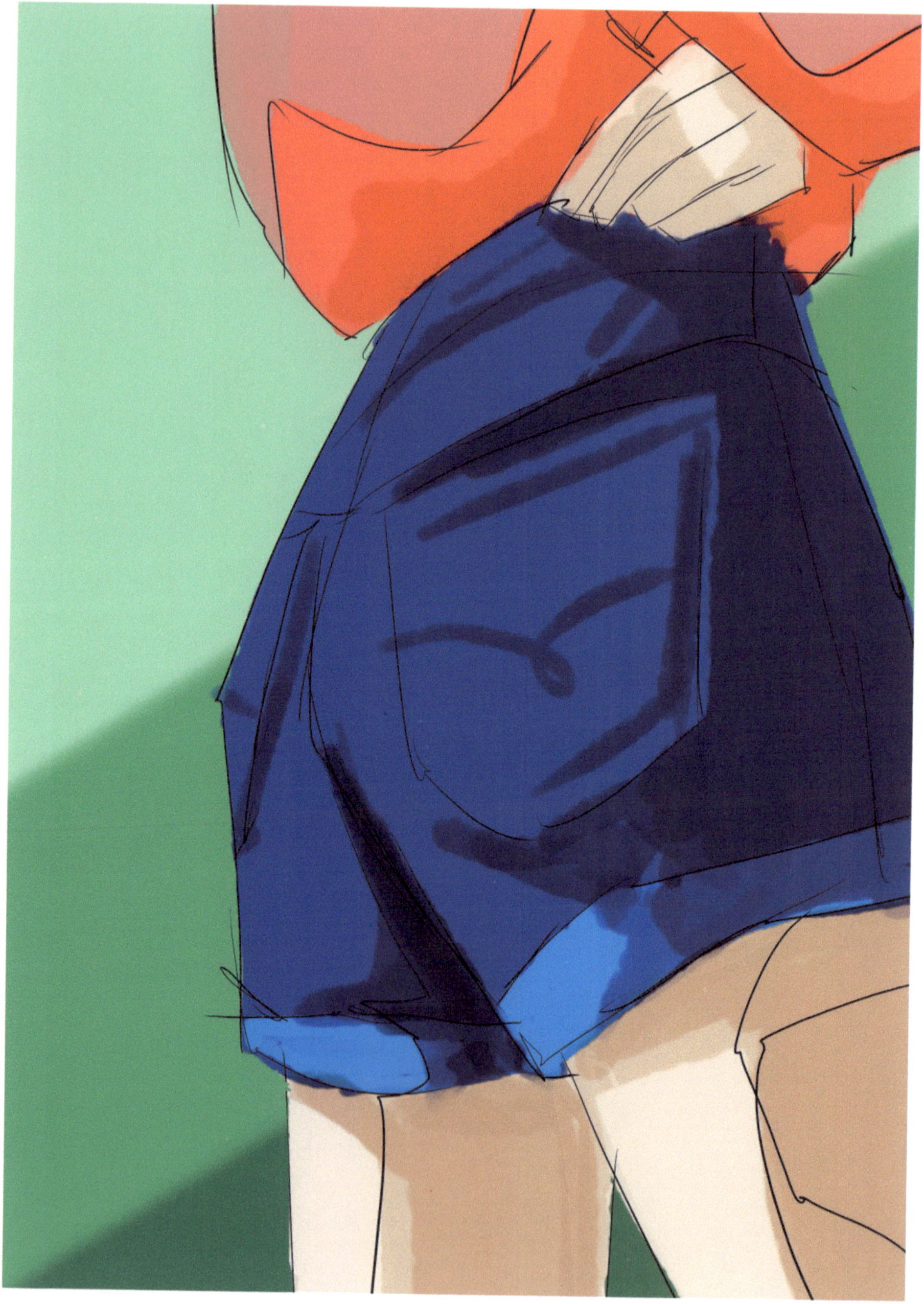

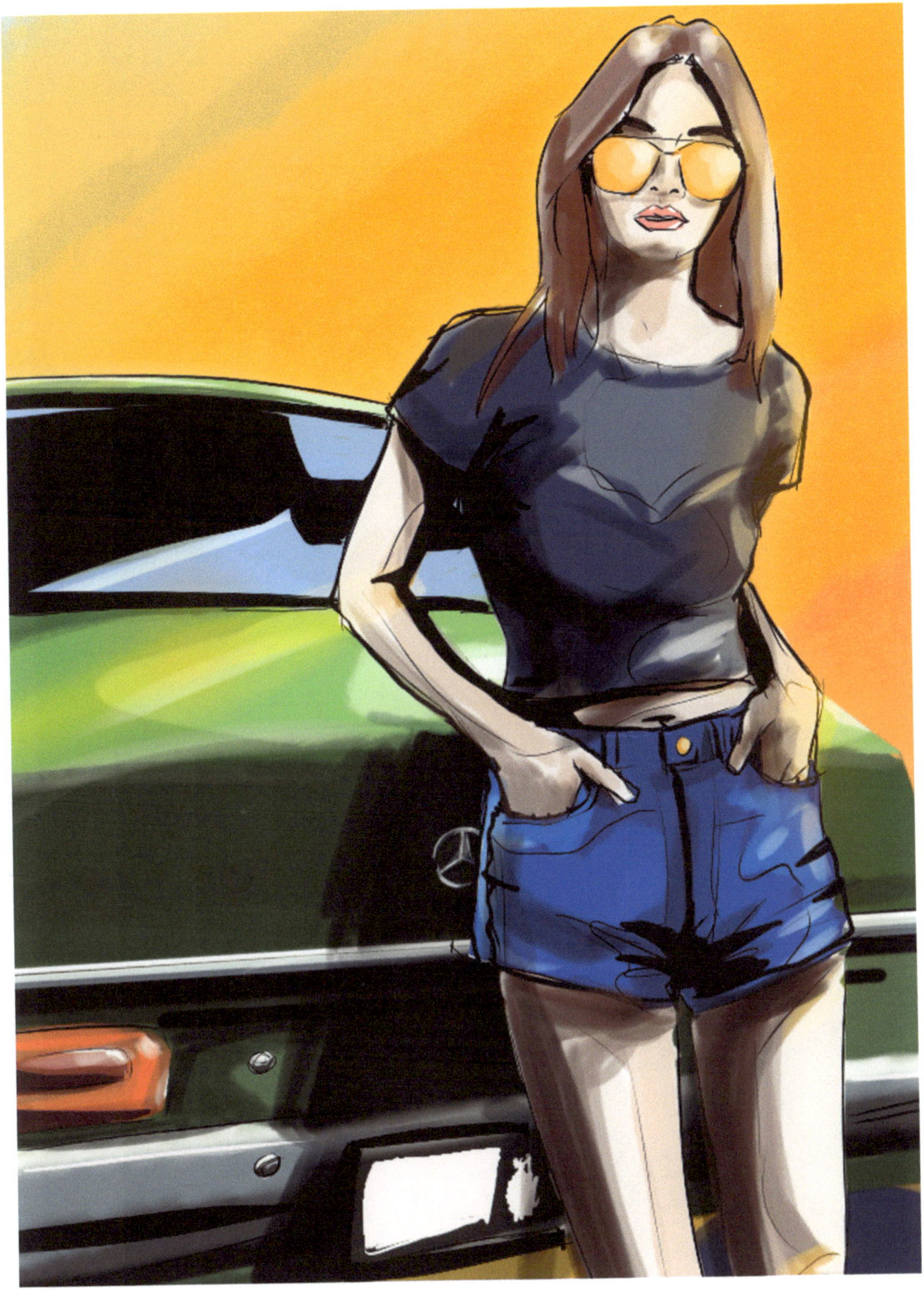

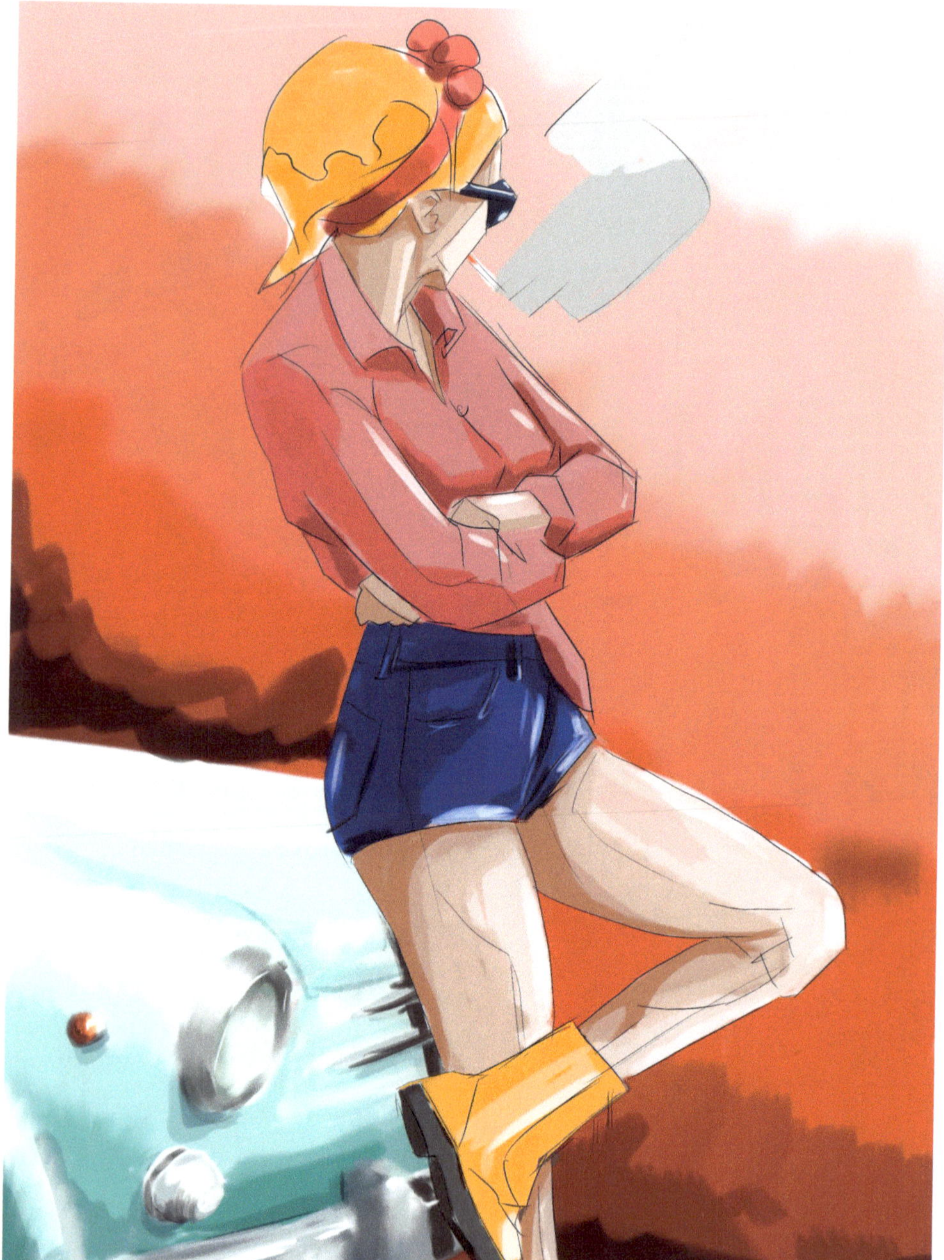

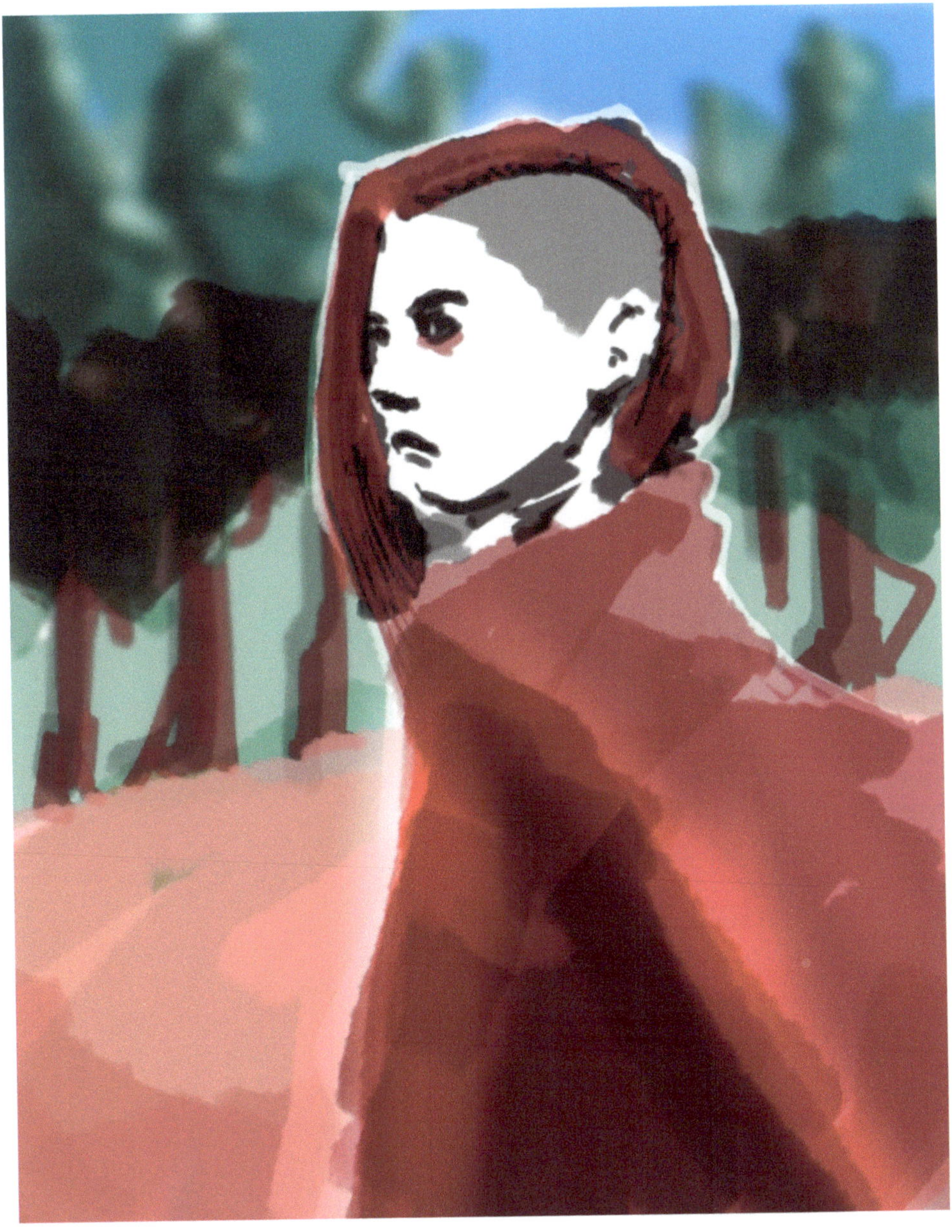

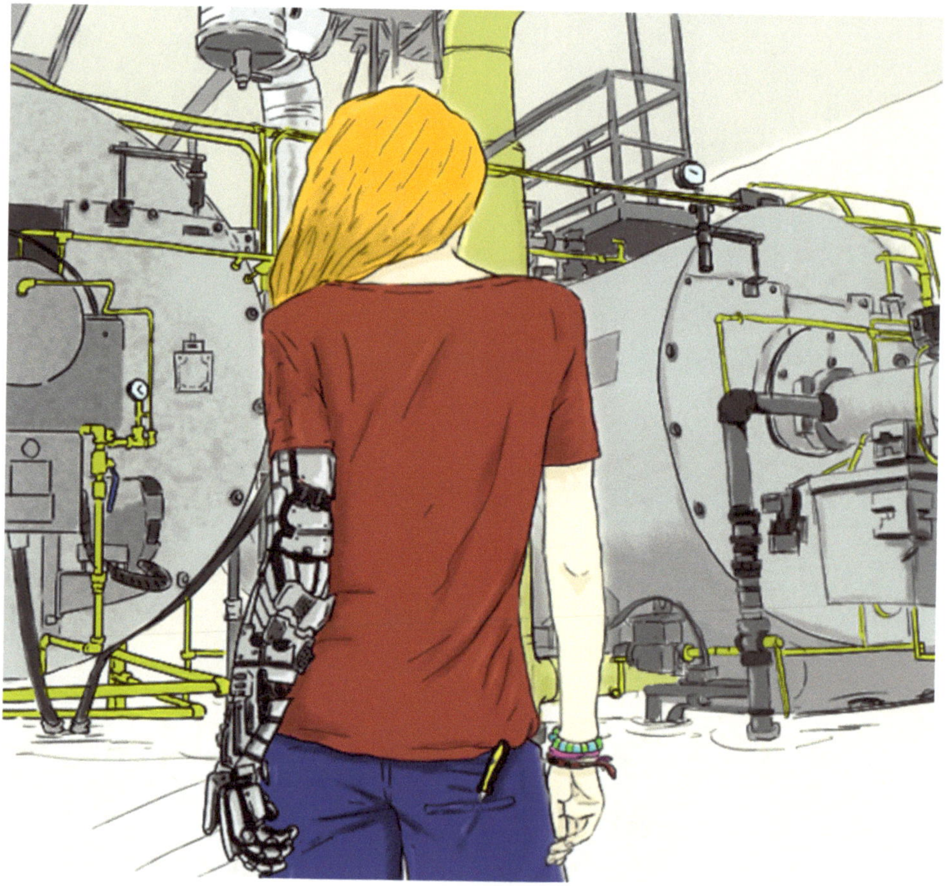

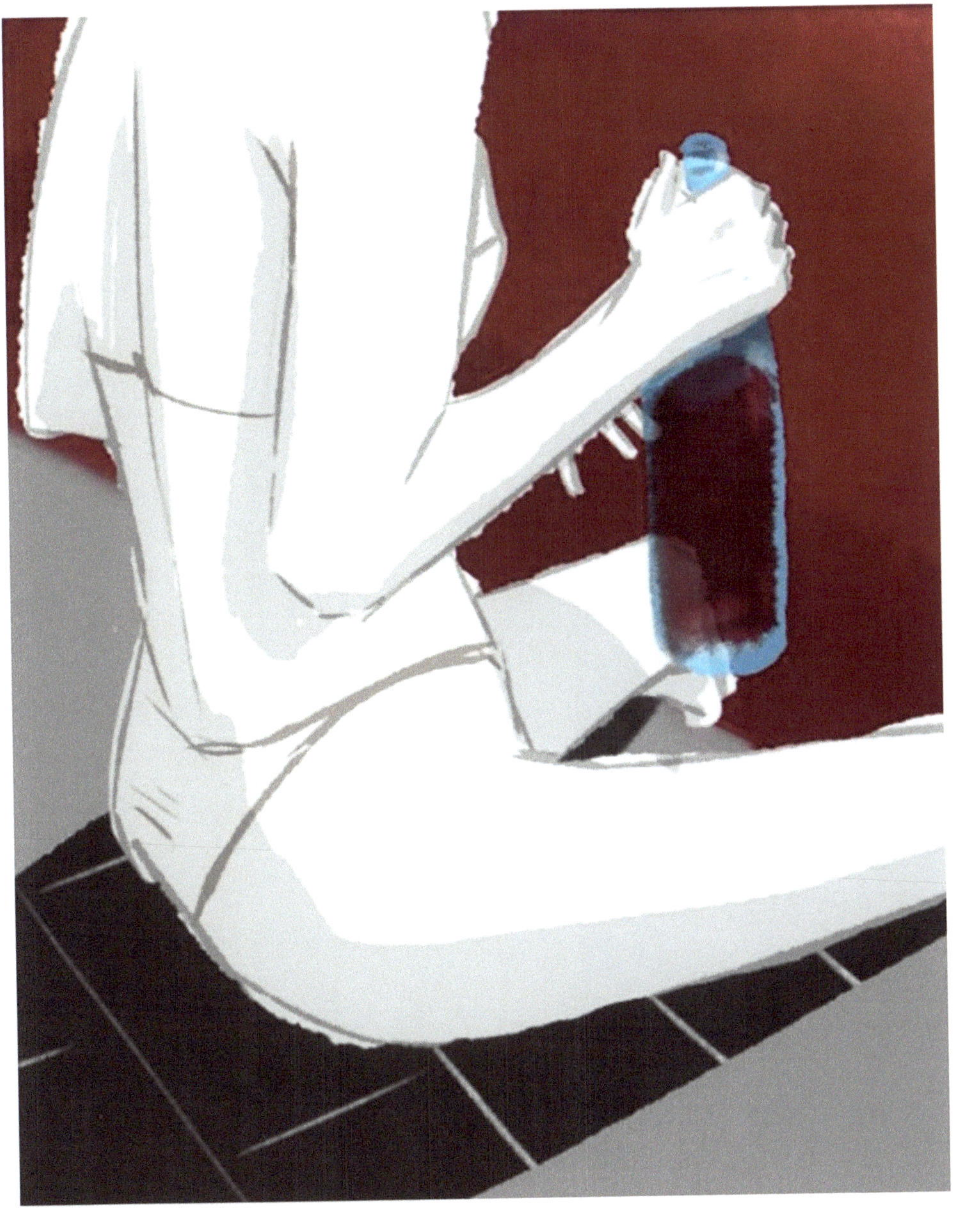

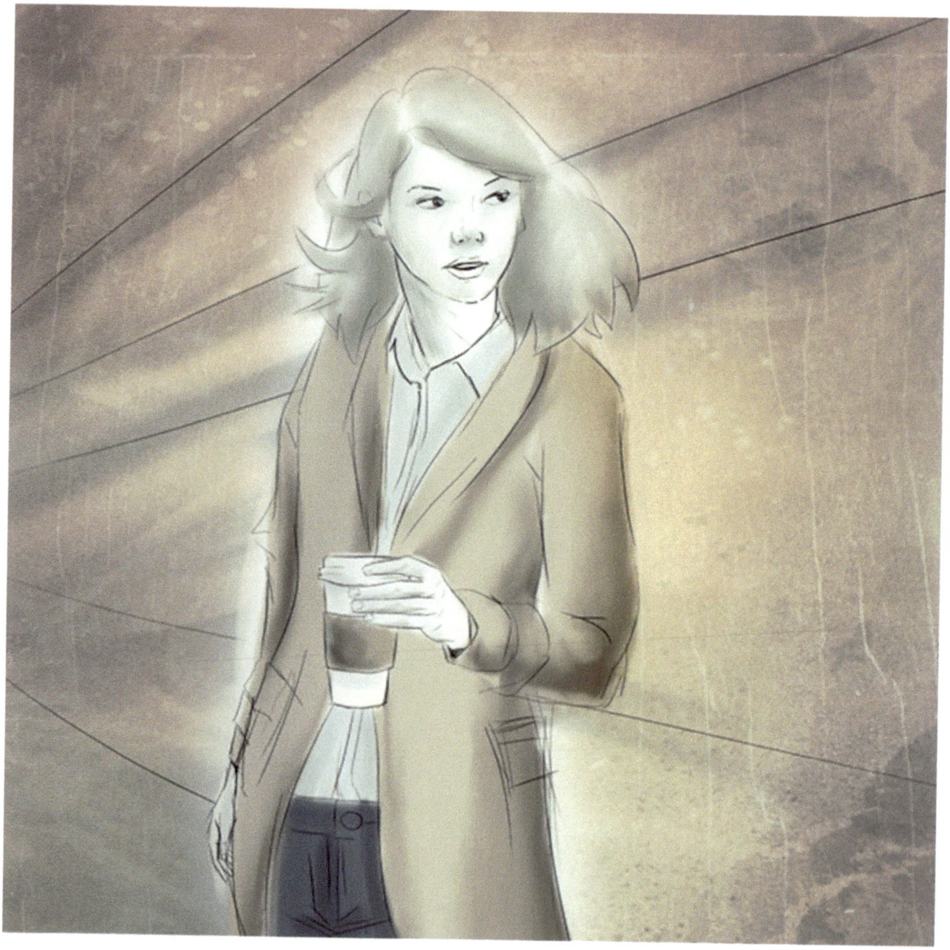

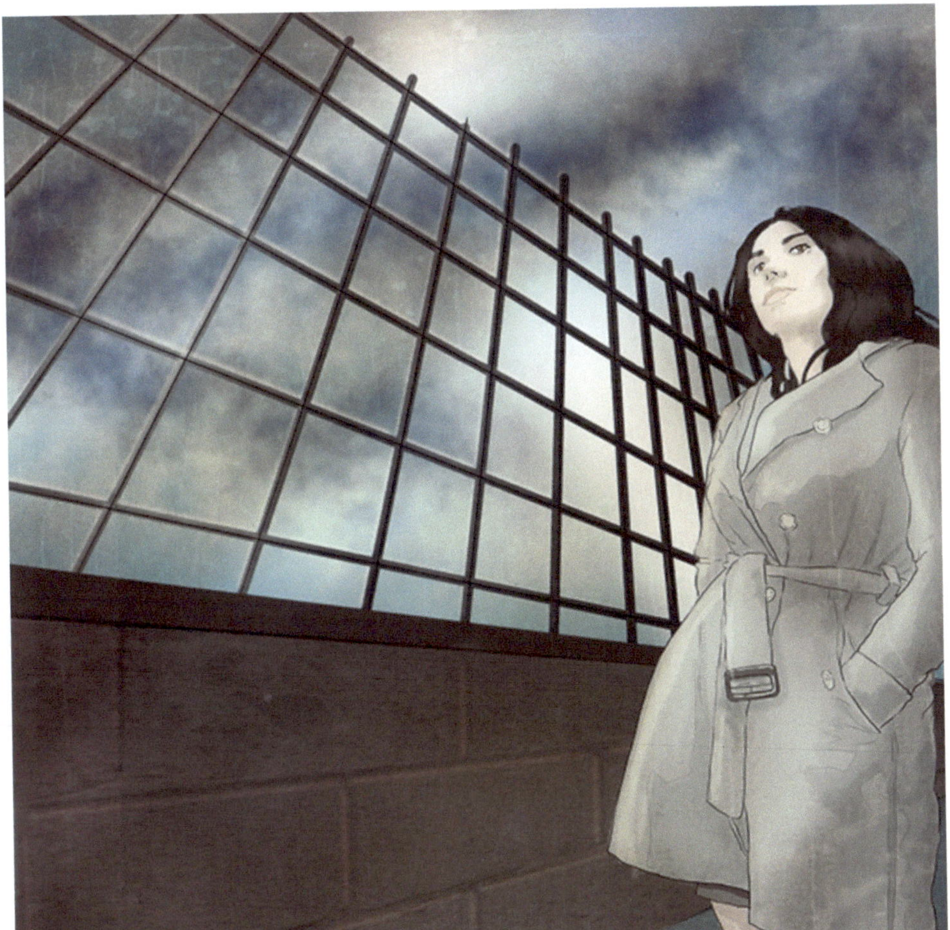

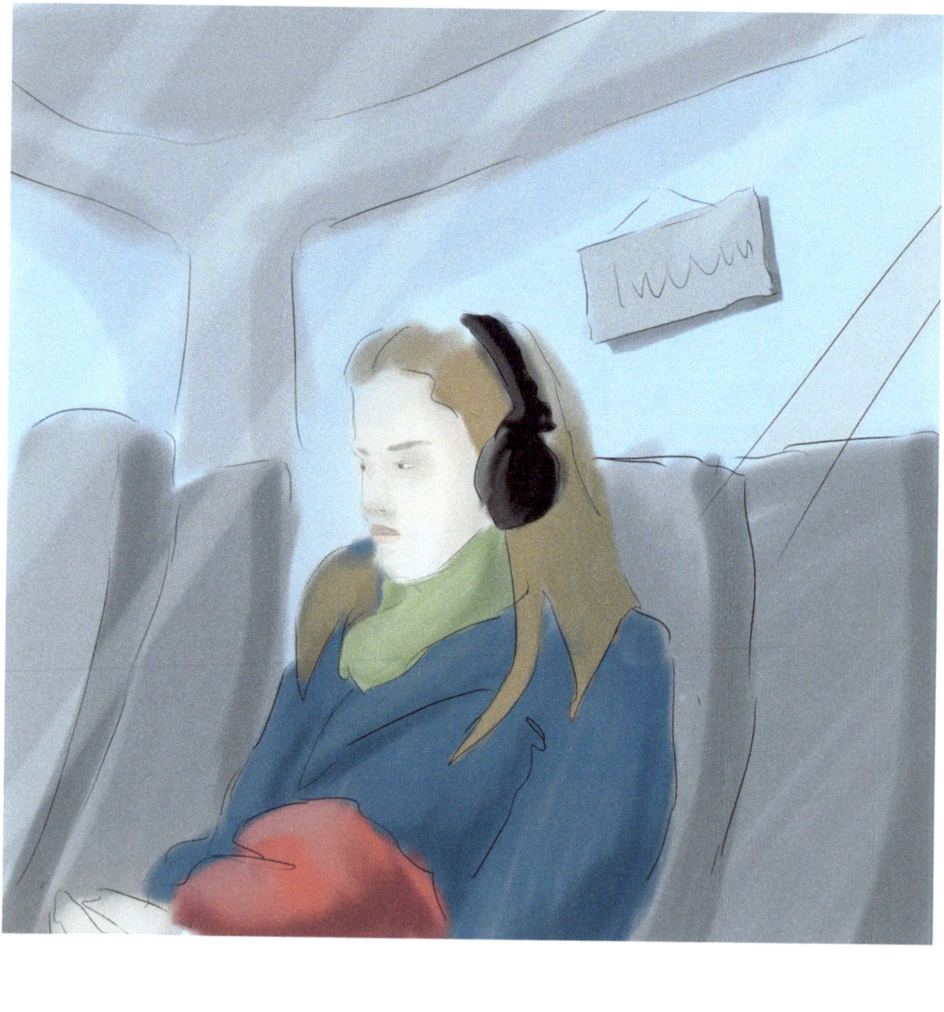

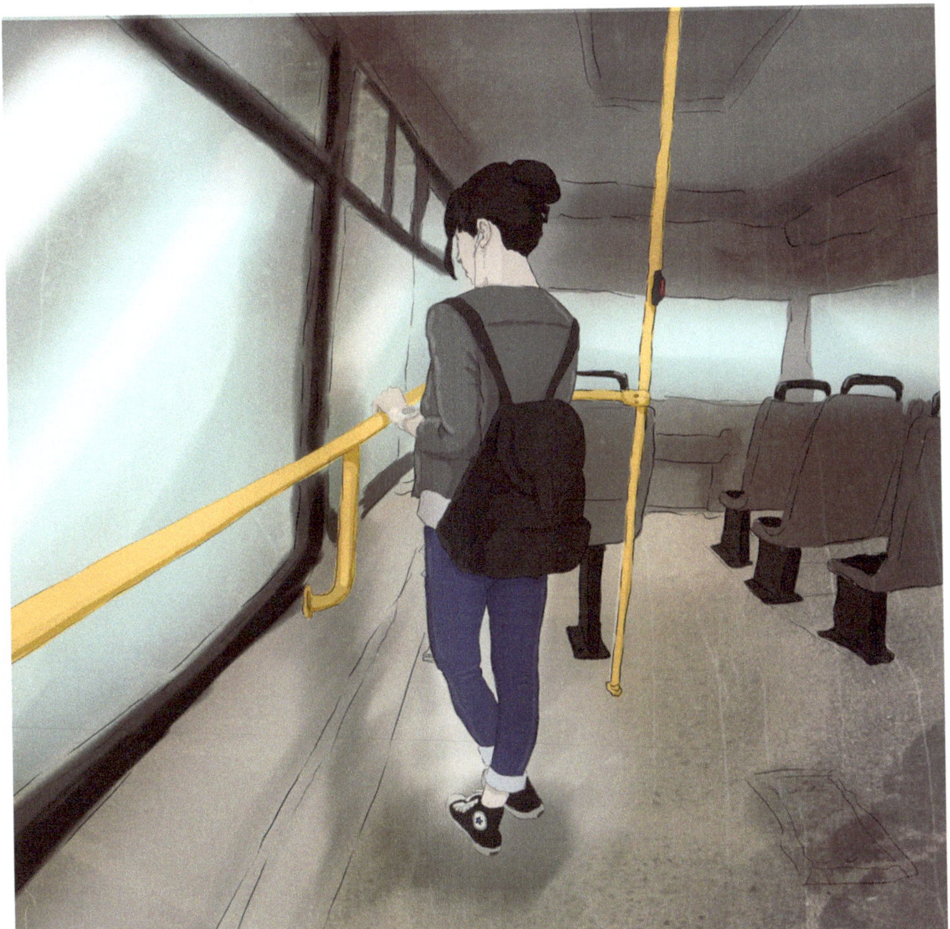

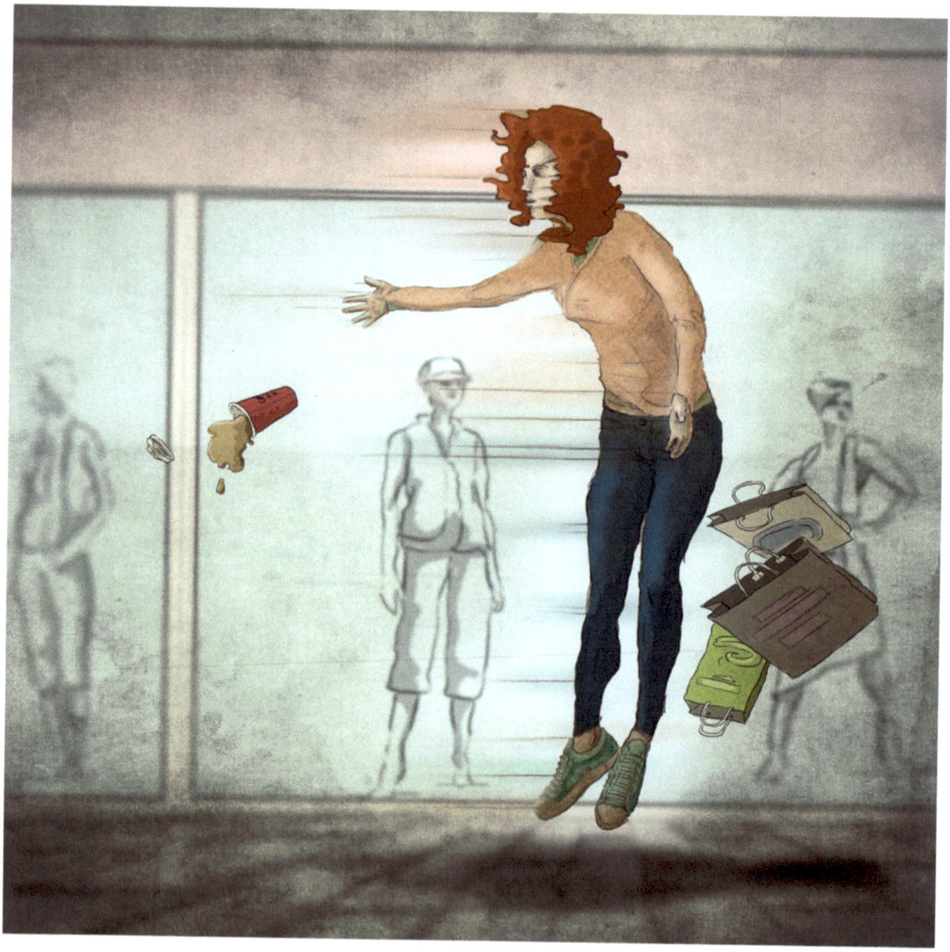

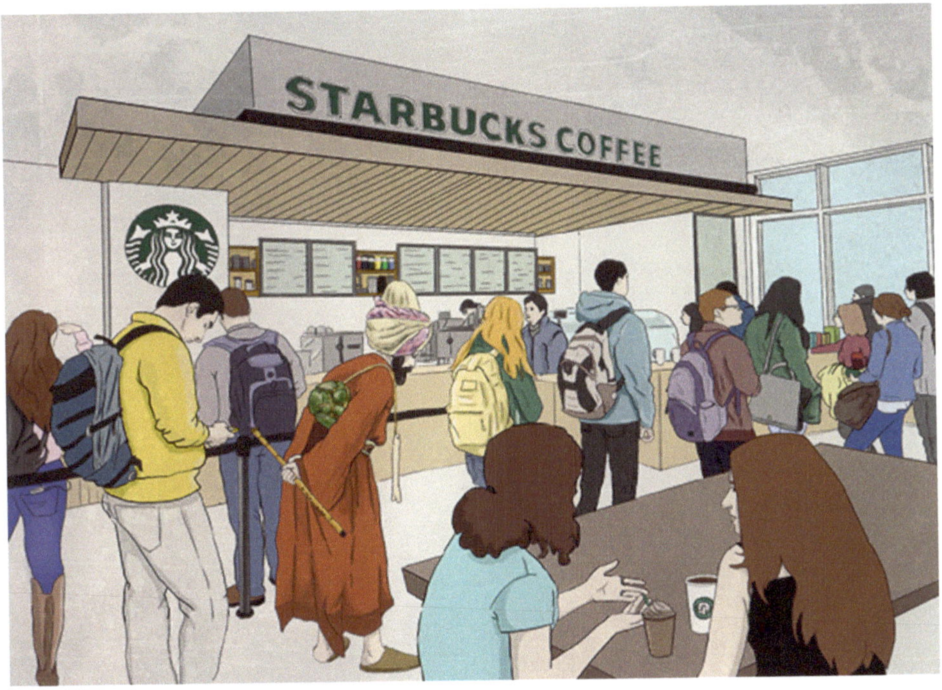
STARBUCKS COFFEE

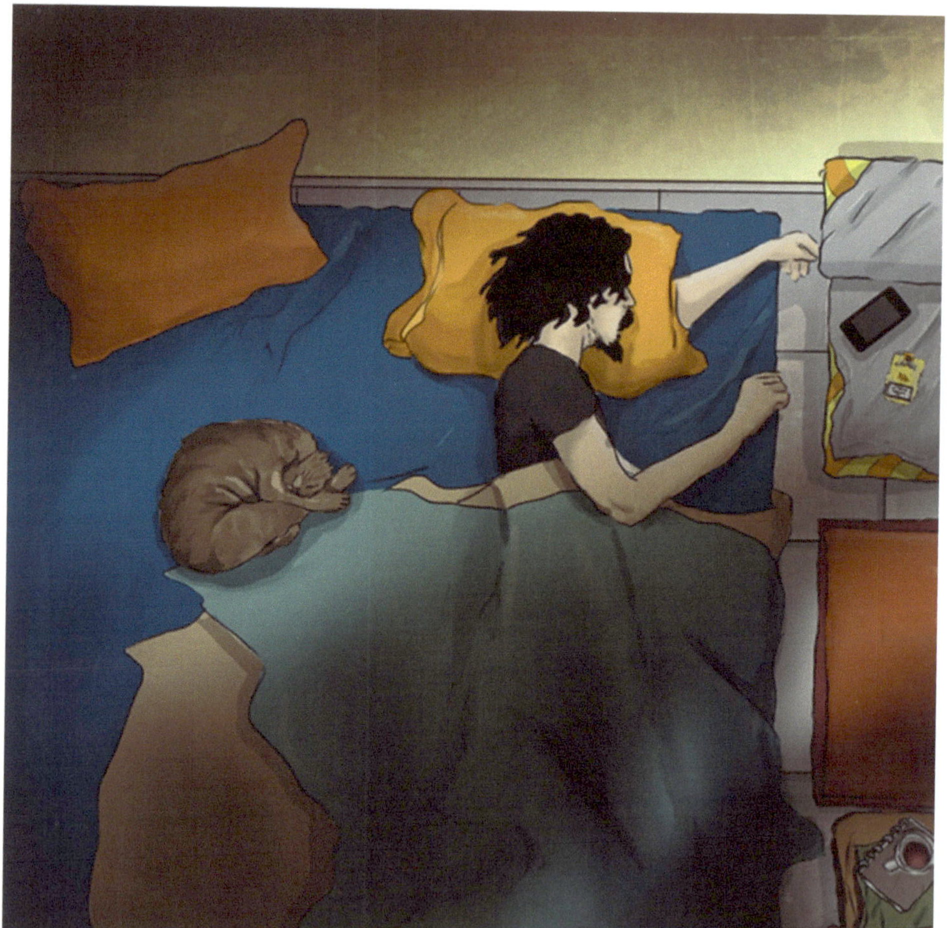

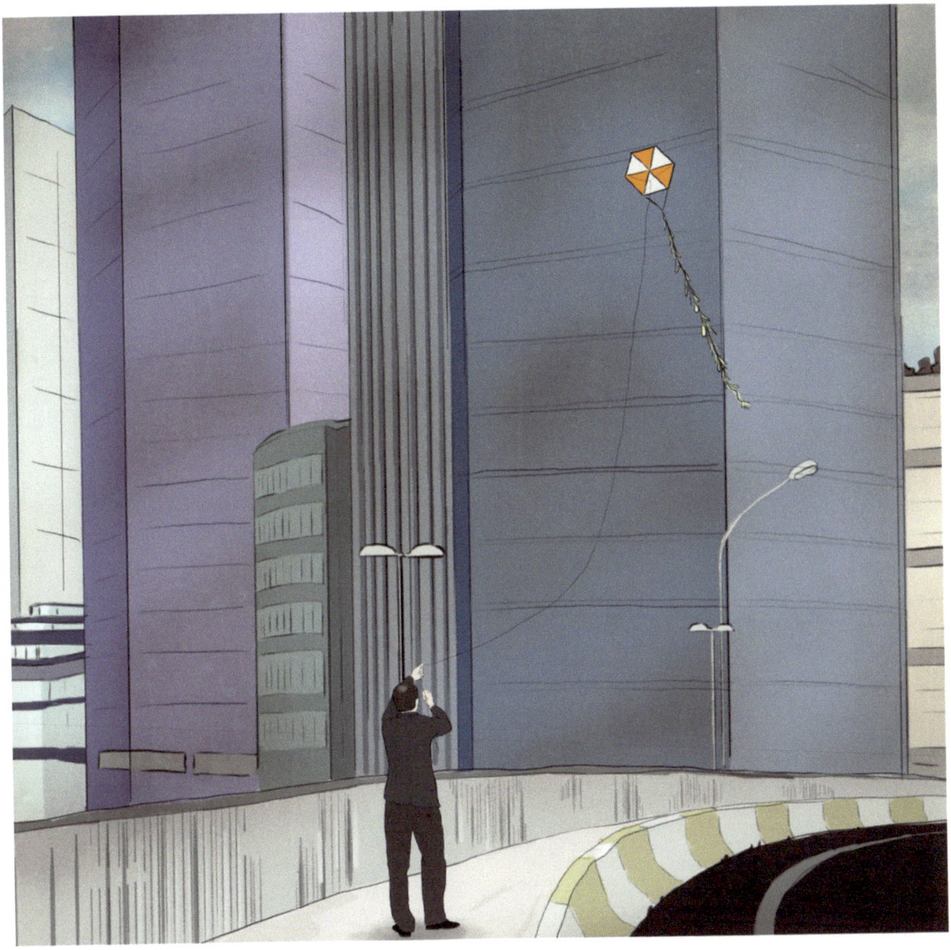

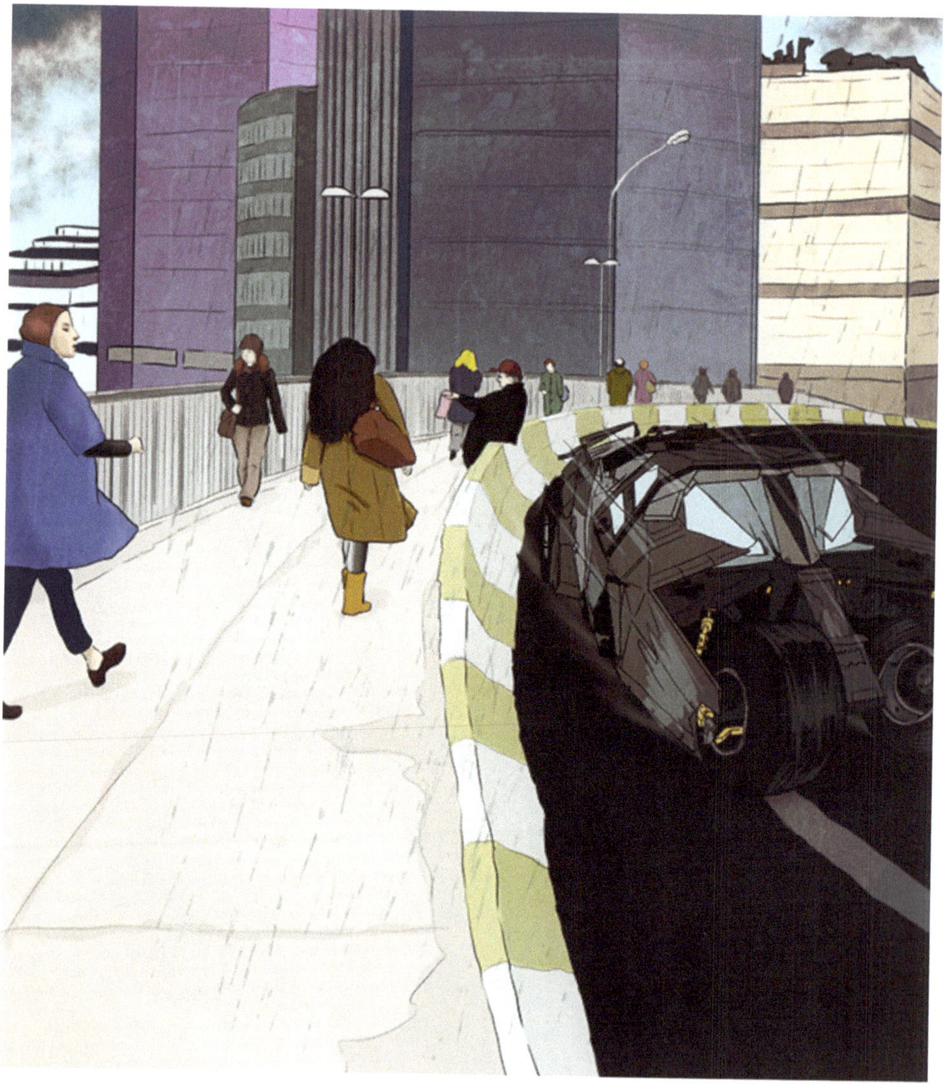

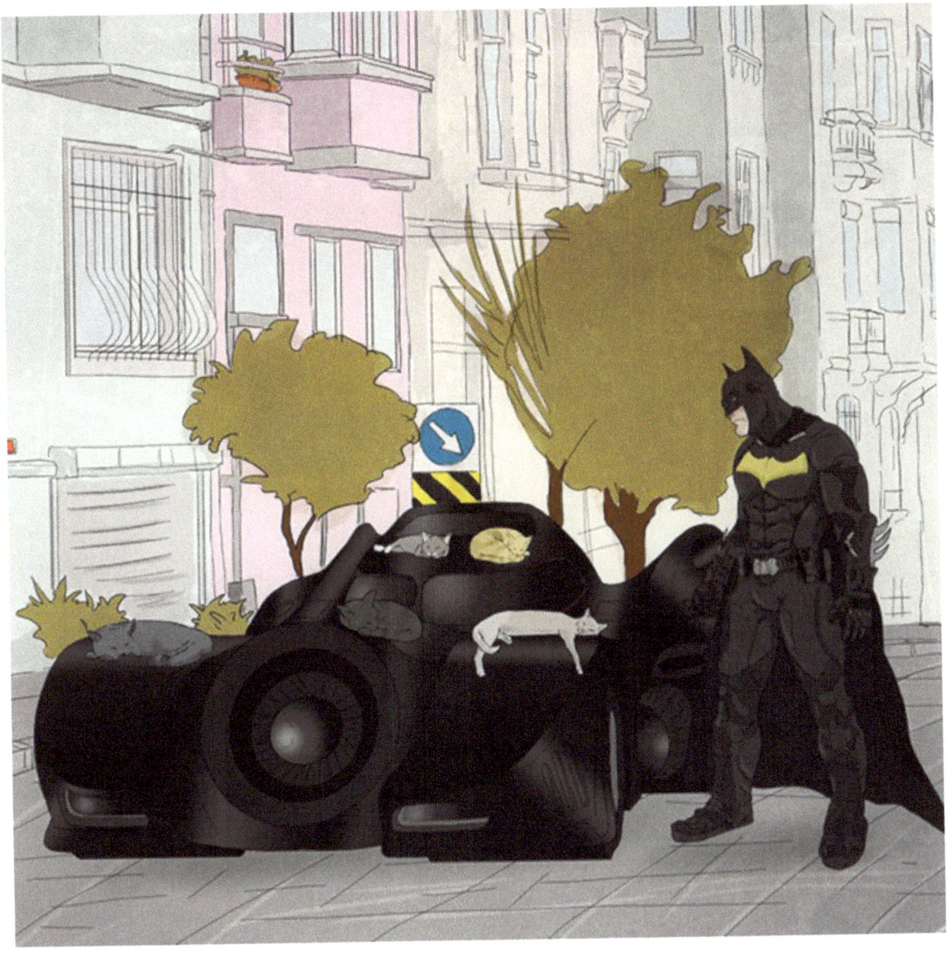

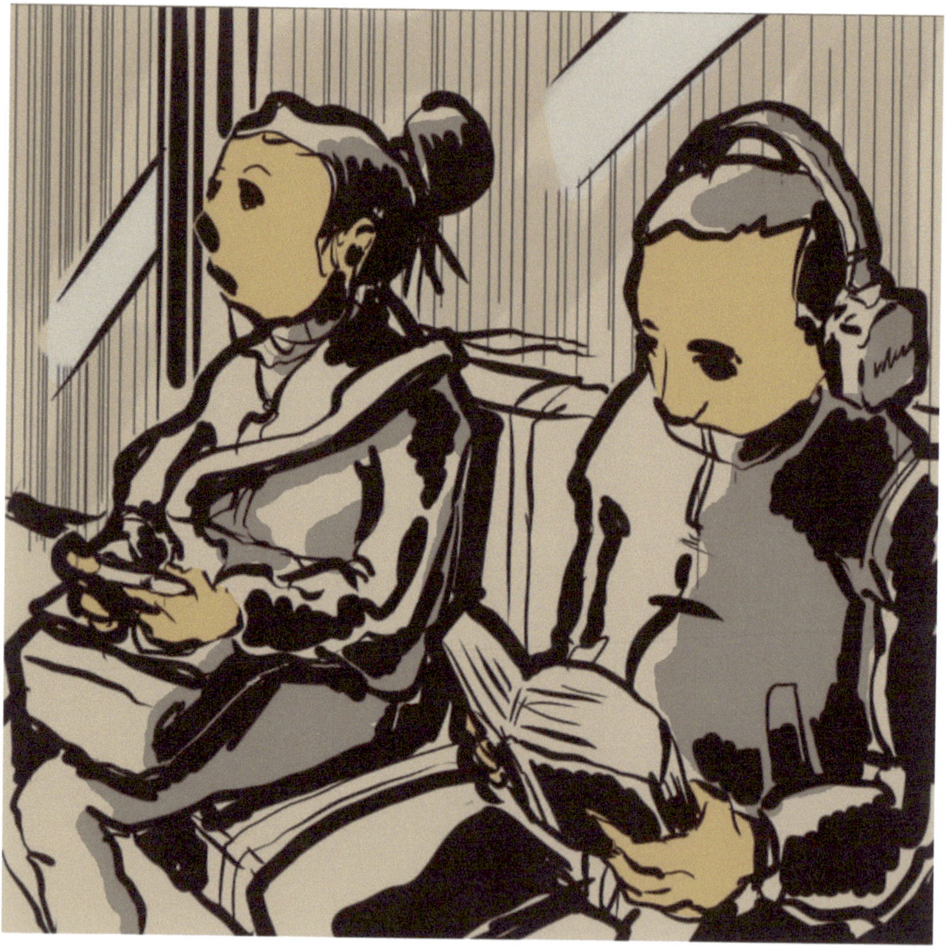

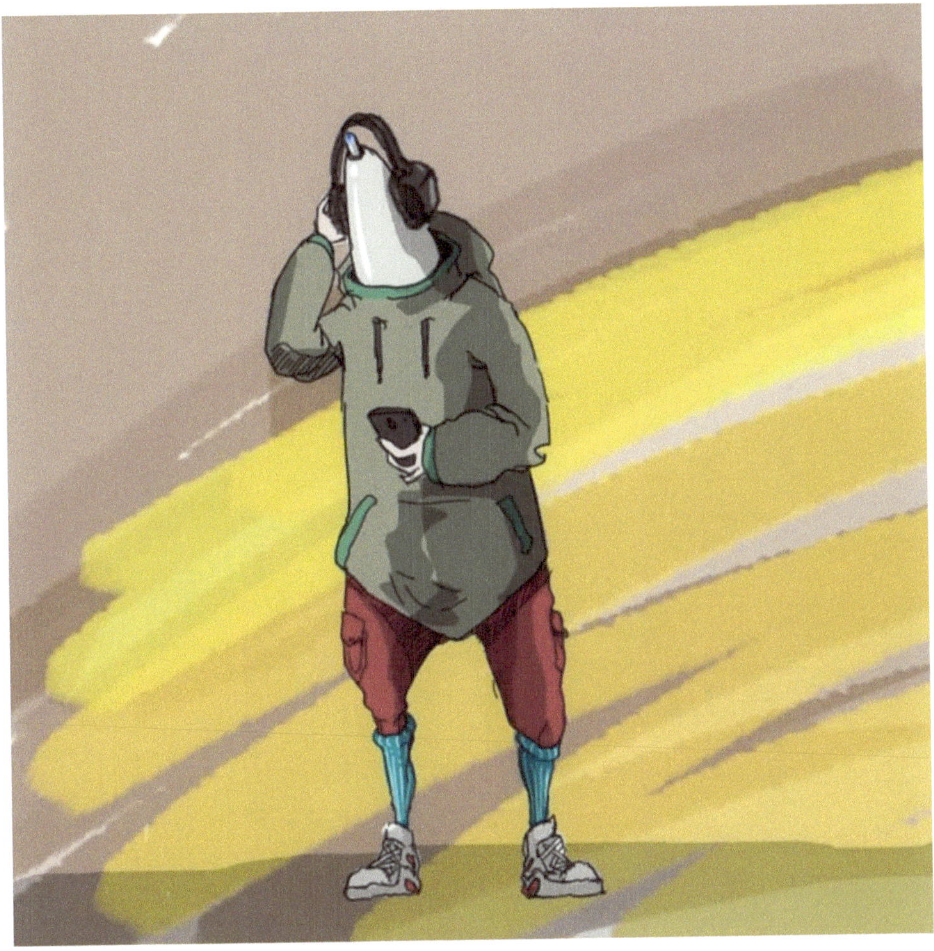

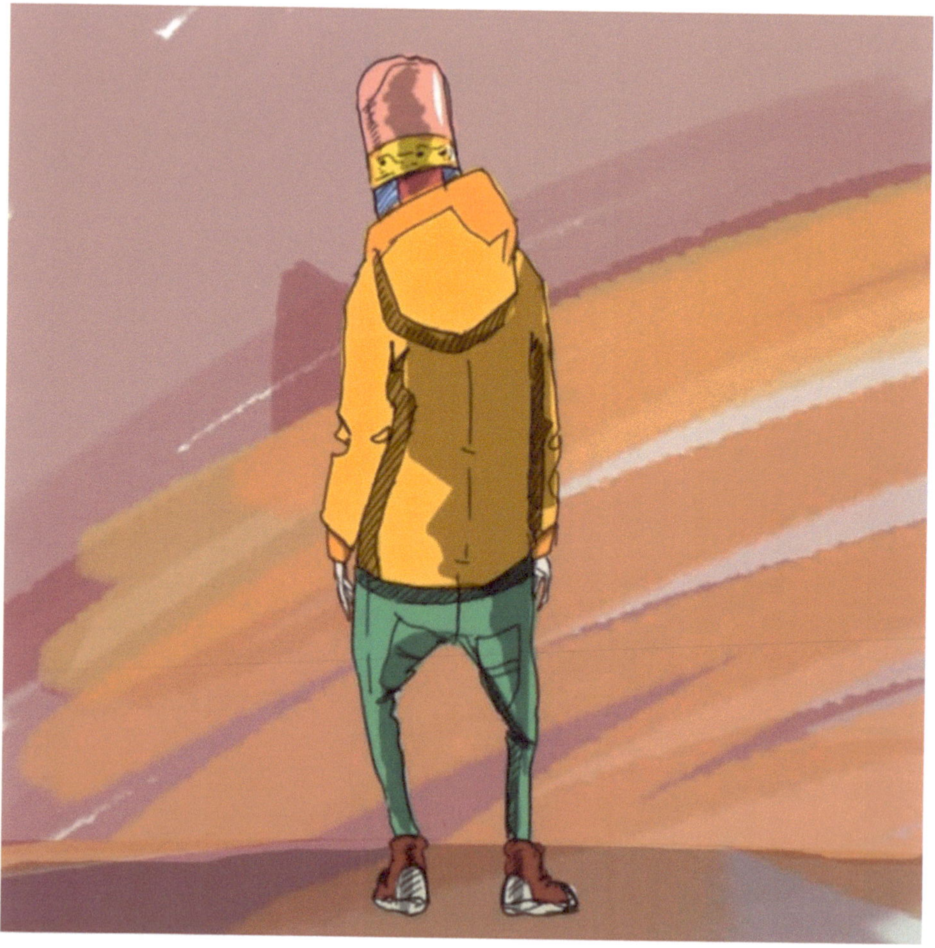

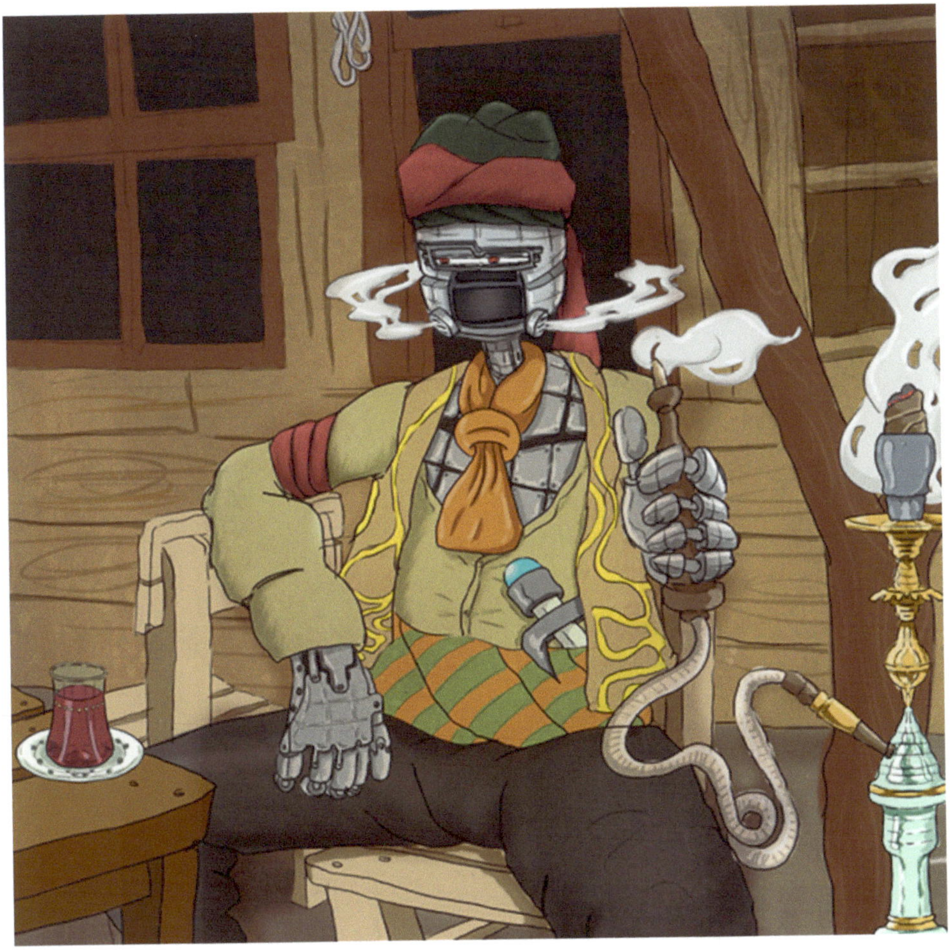

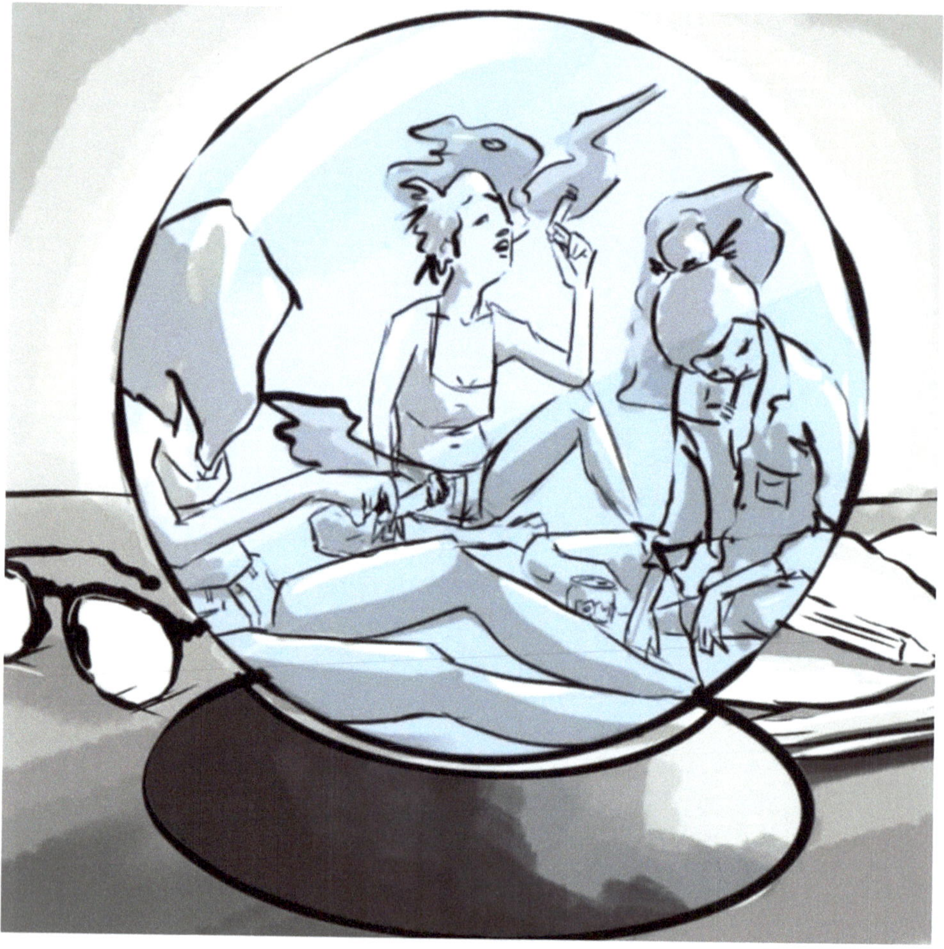

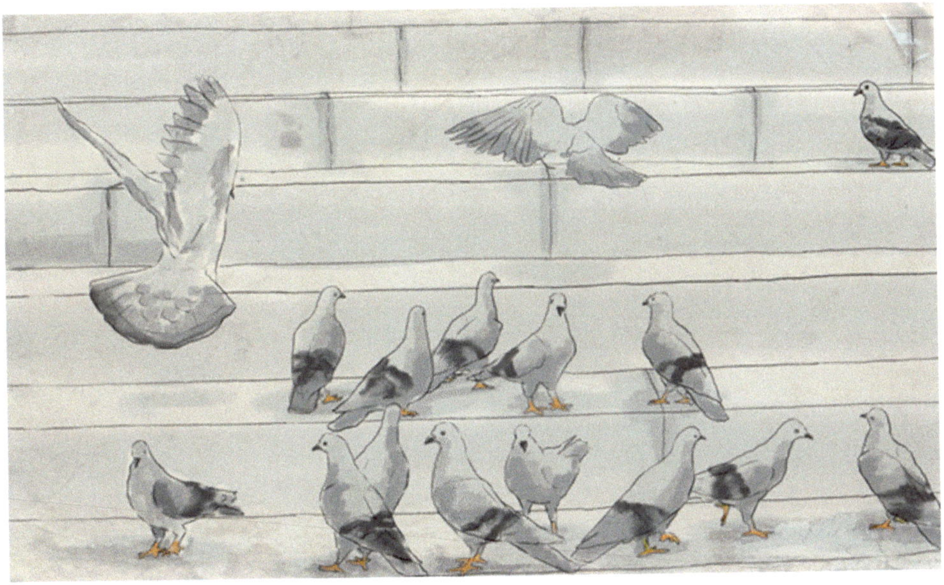

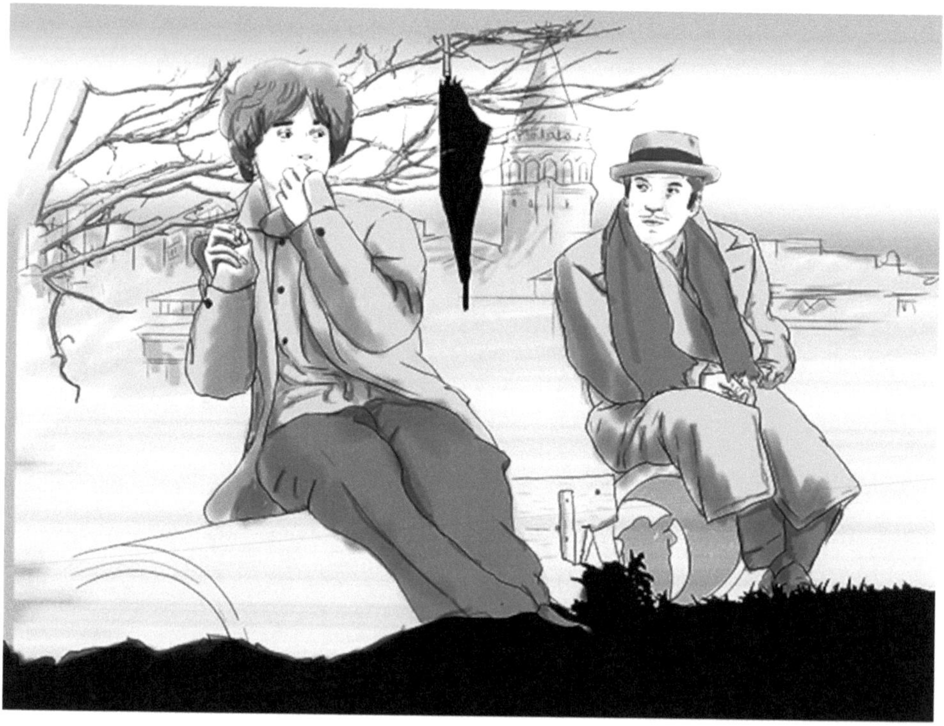

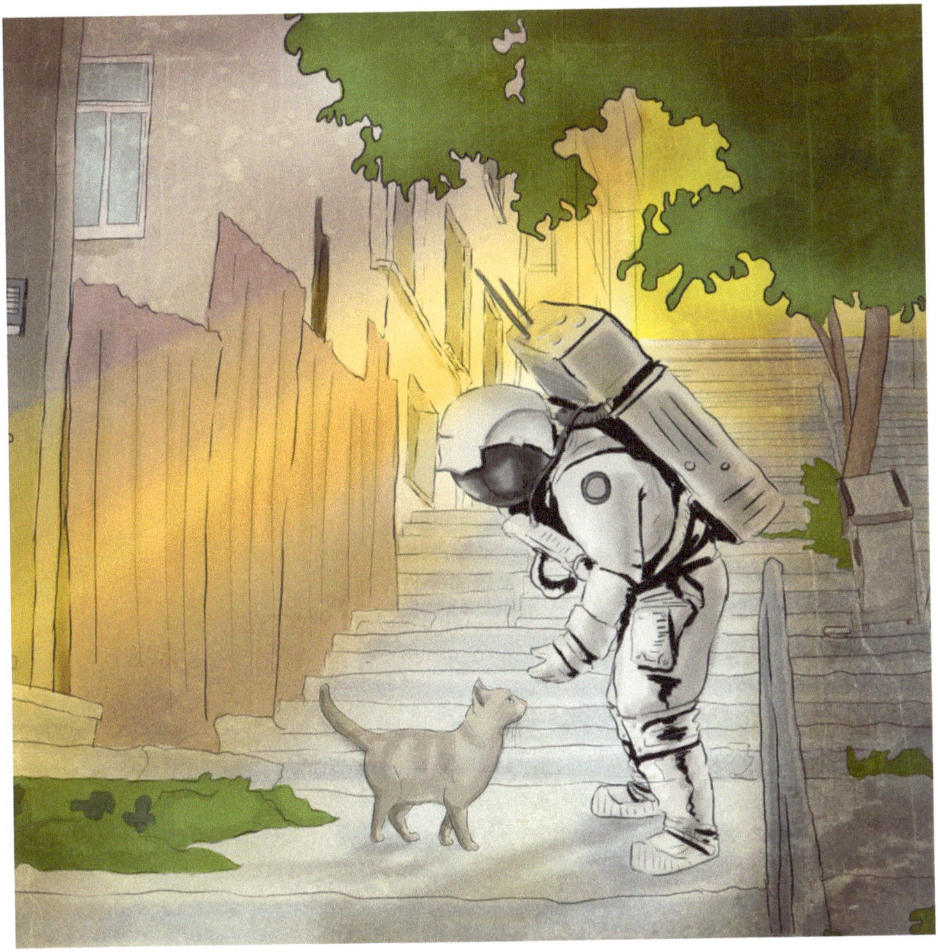

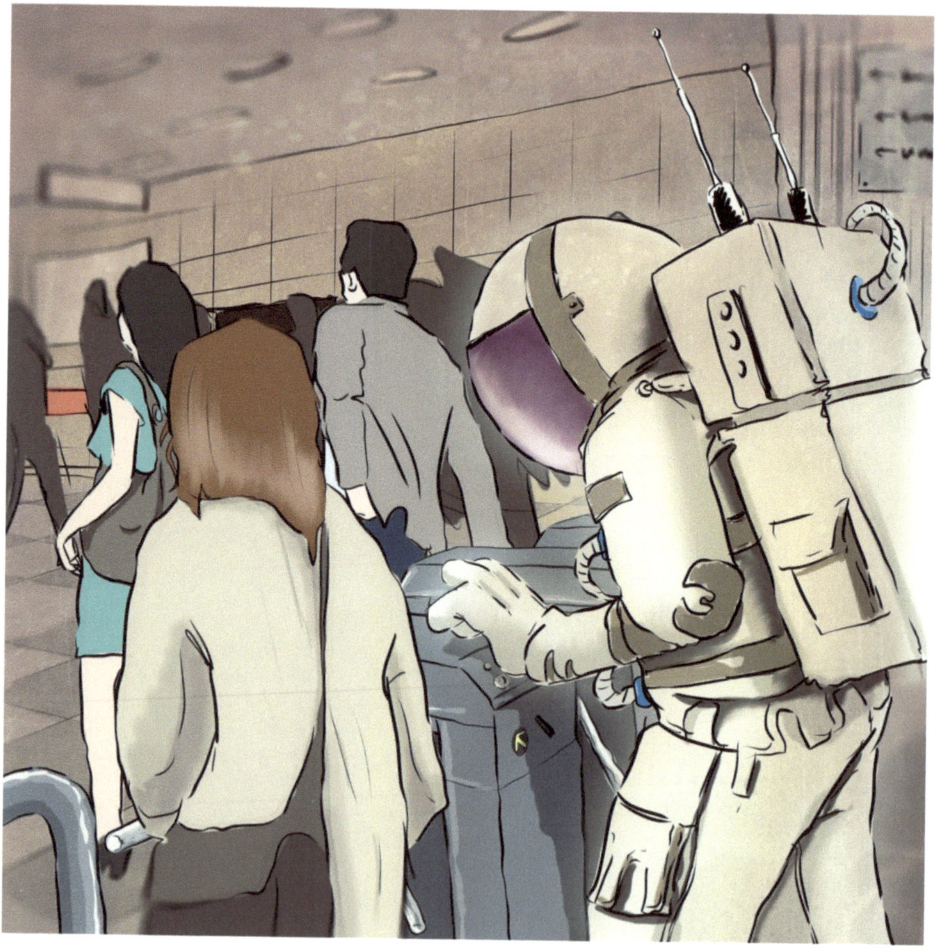

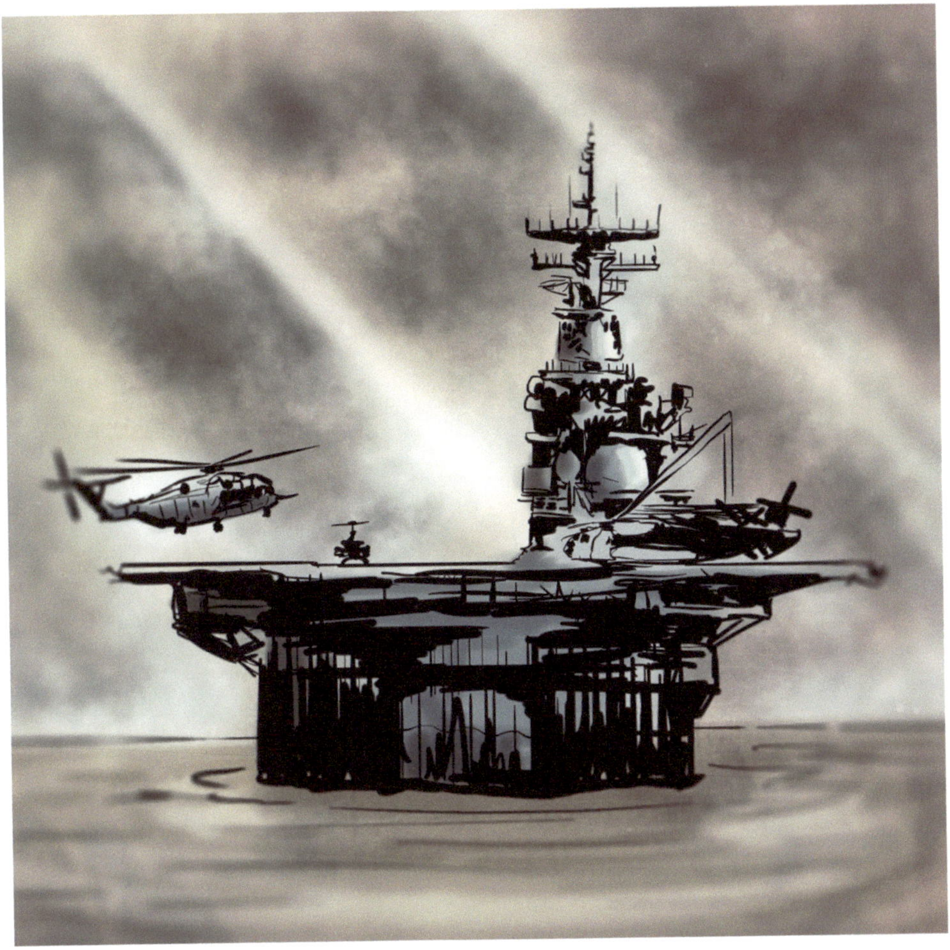

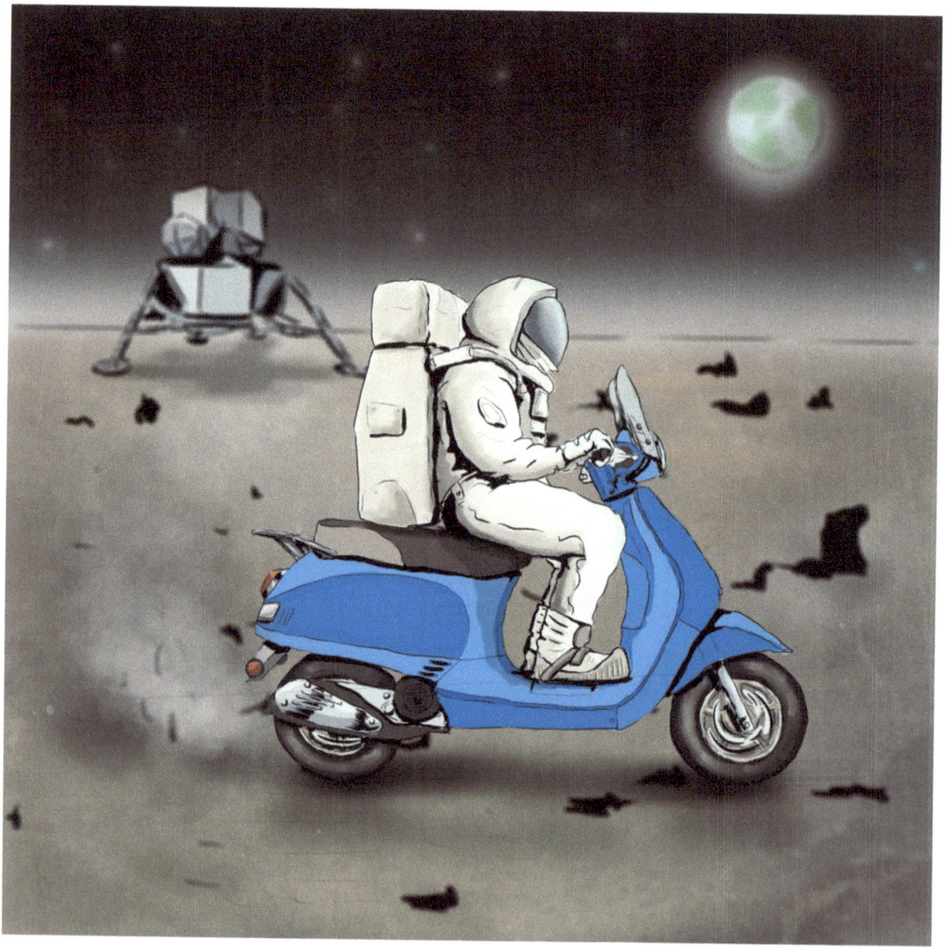

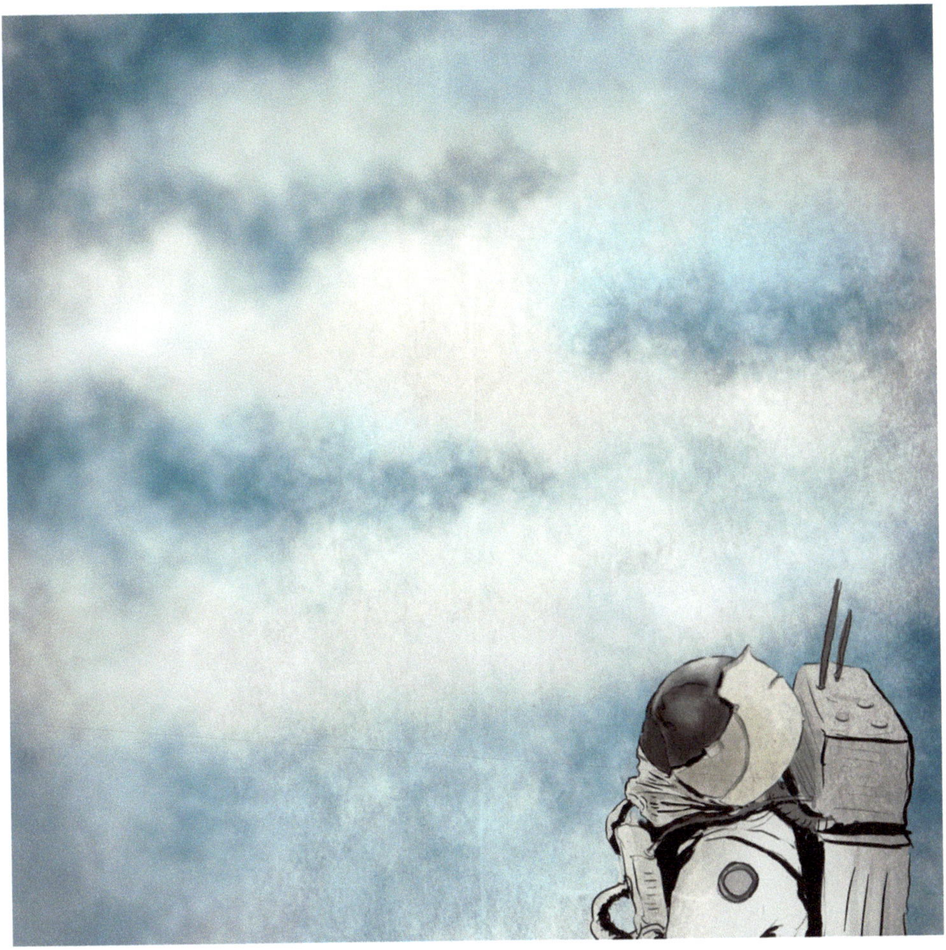

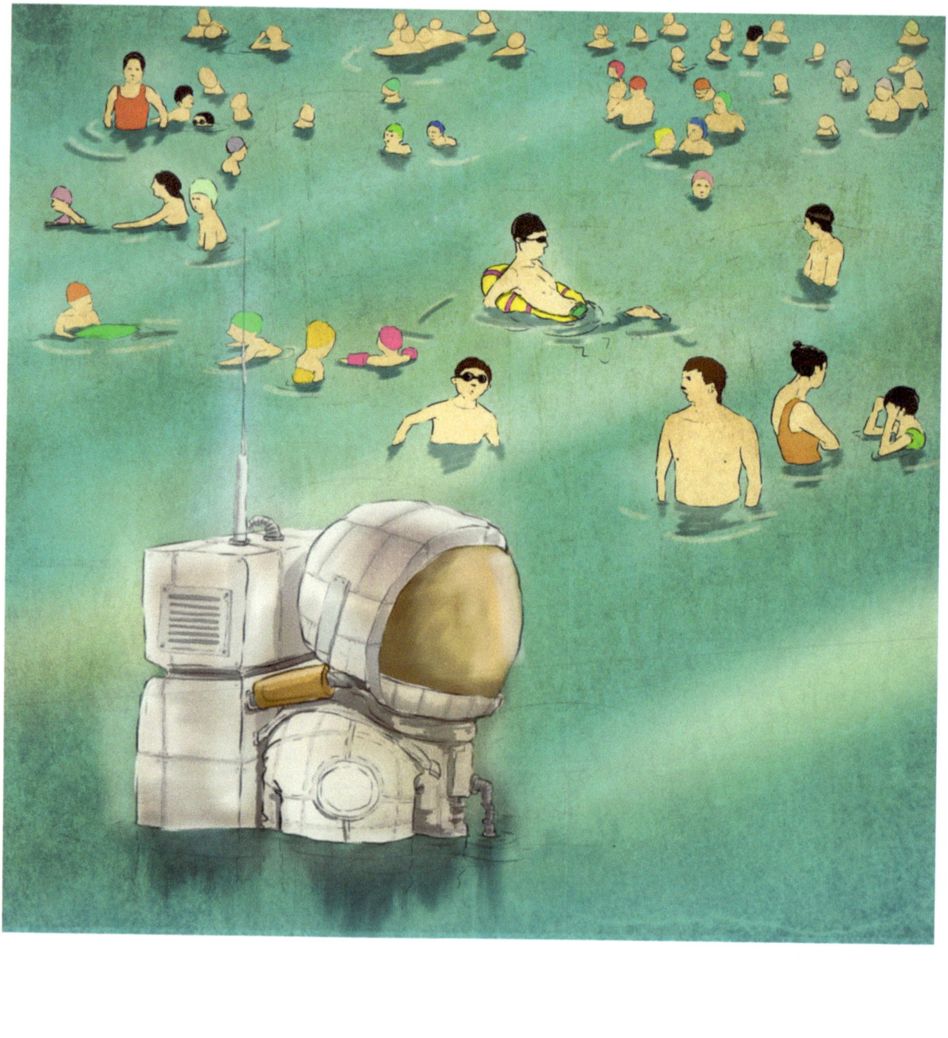

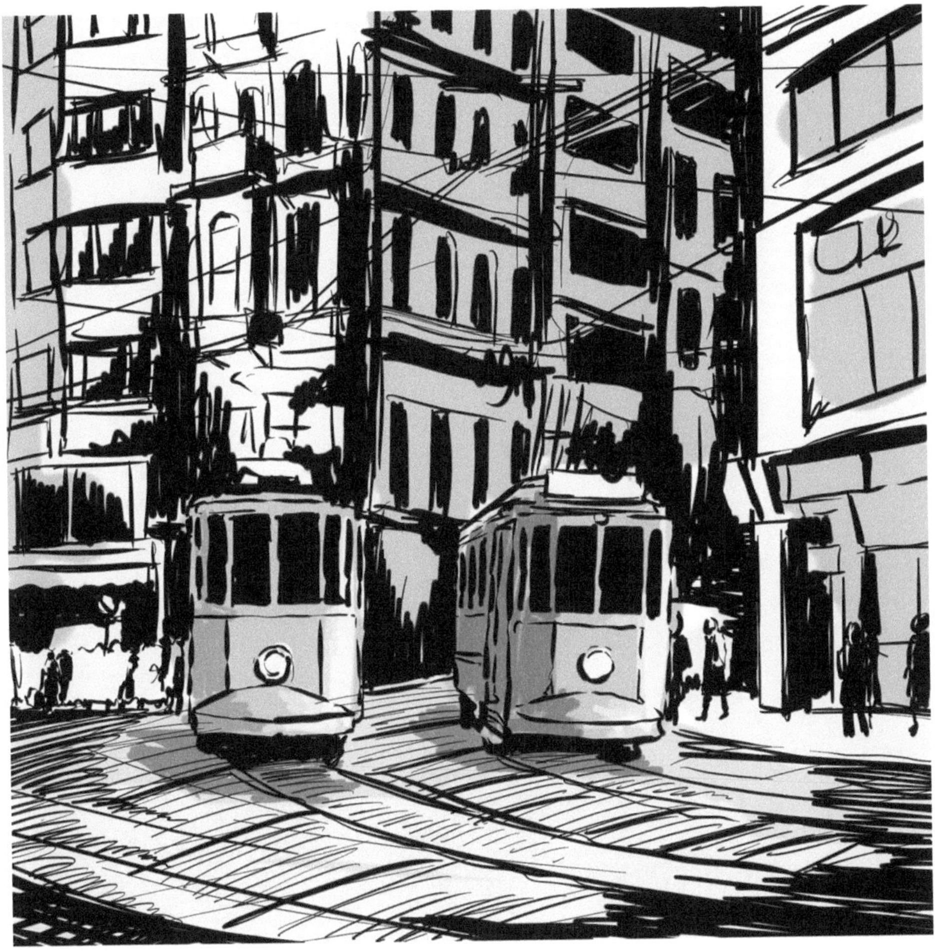

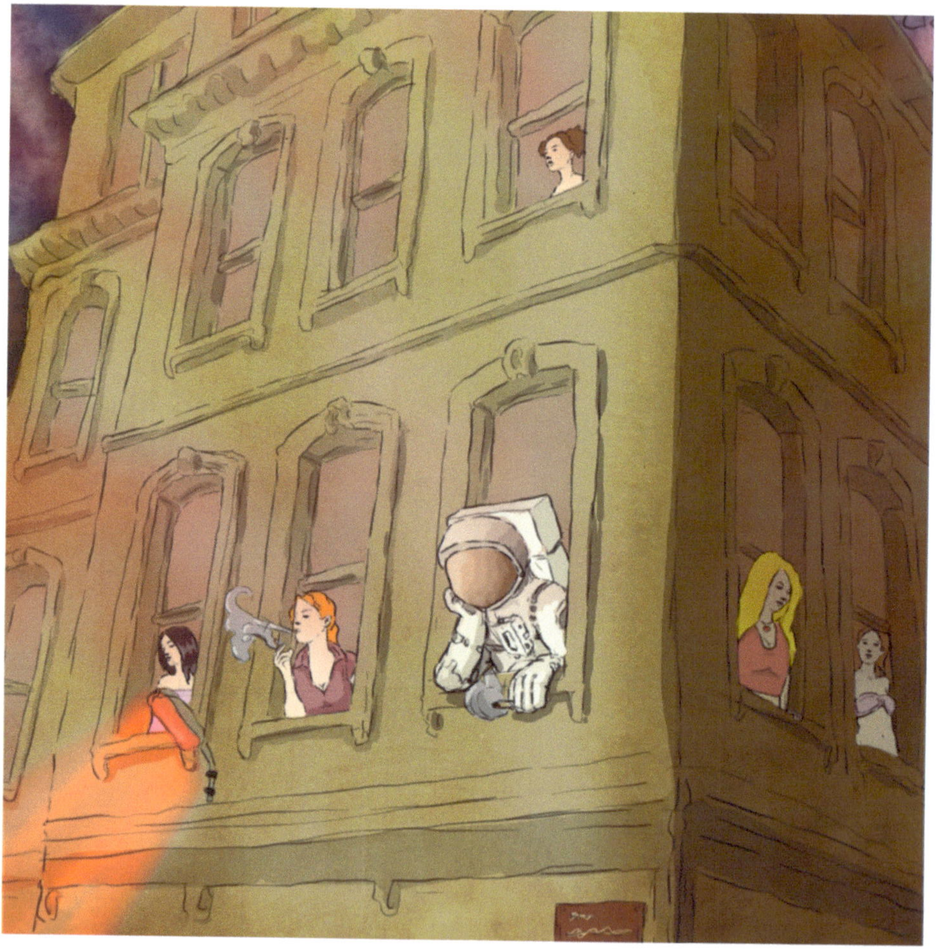

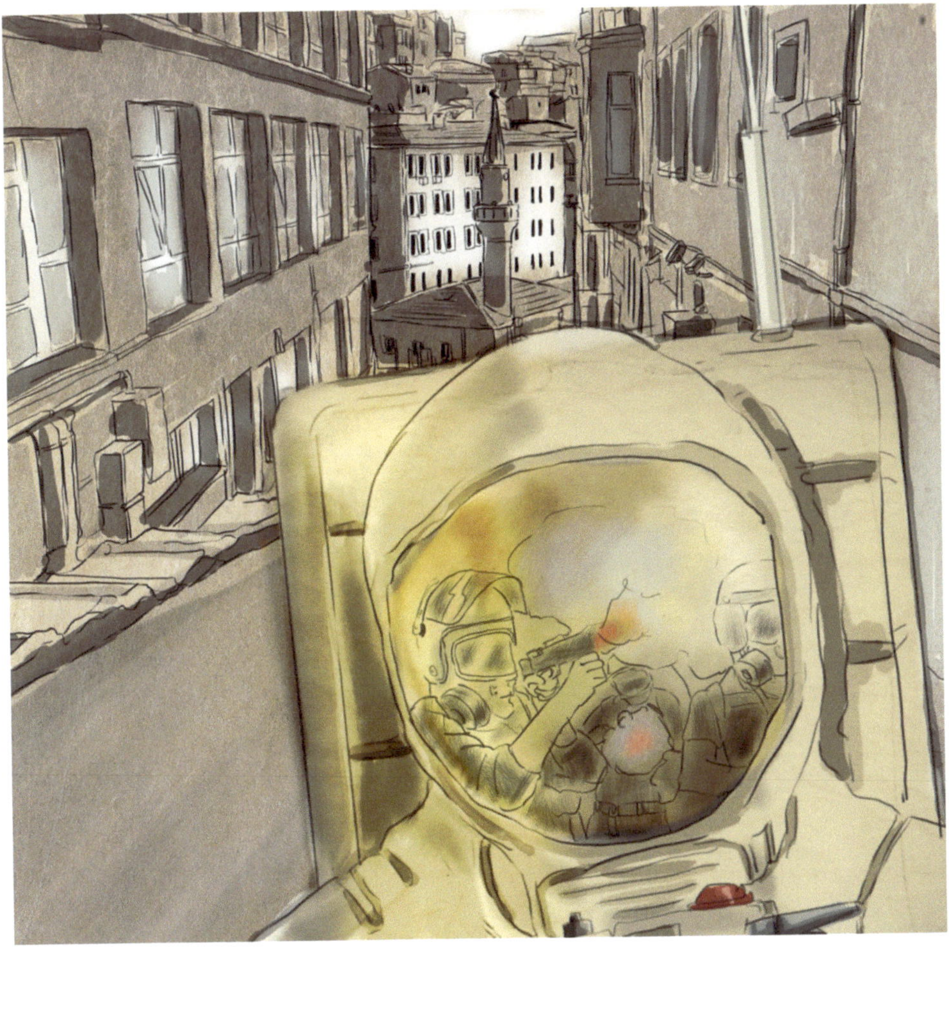

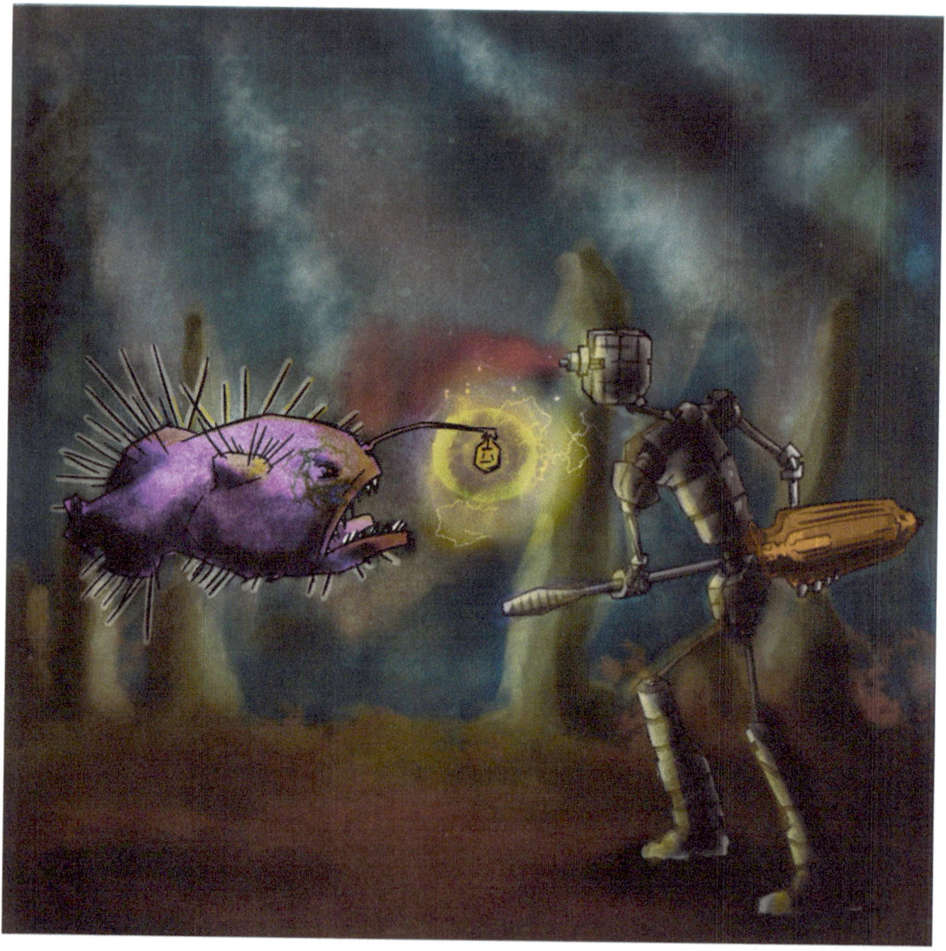

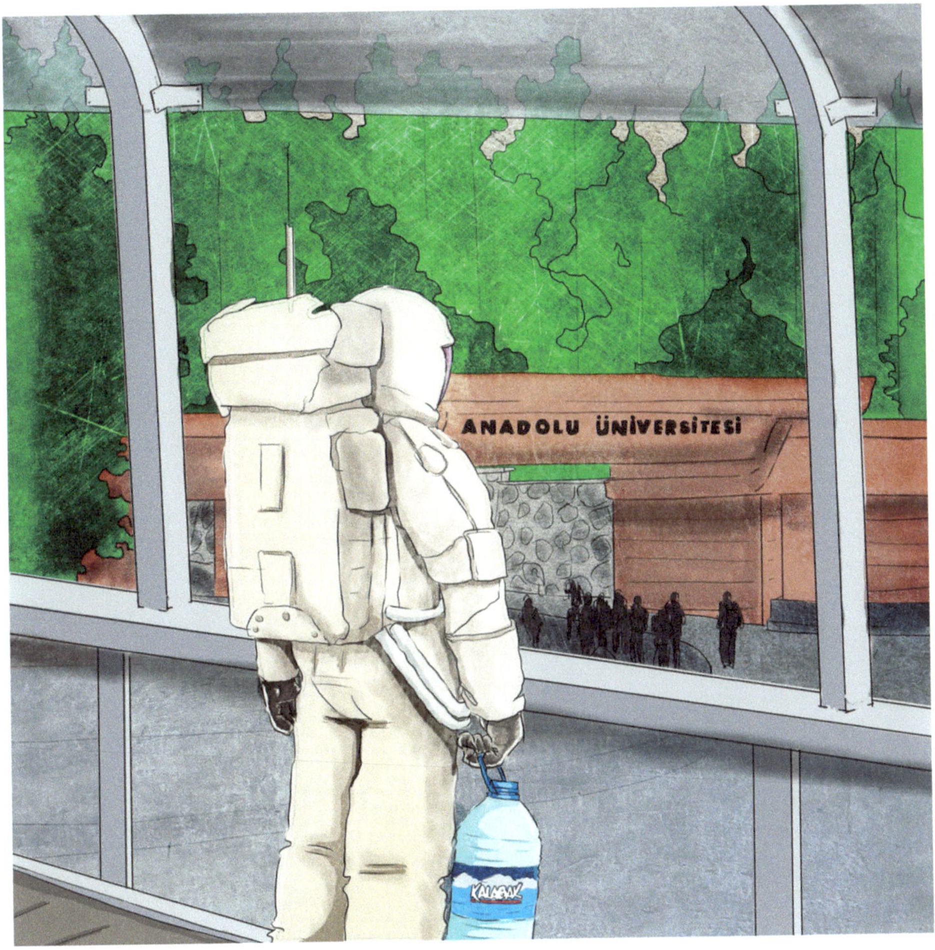
ANADOLU ÜNİVERSİTESİ
KALABAK

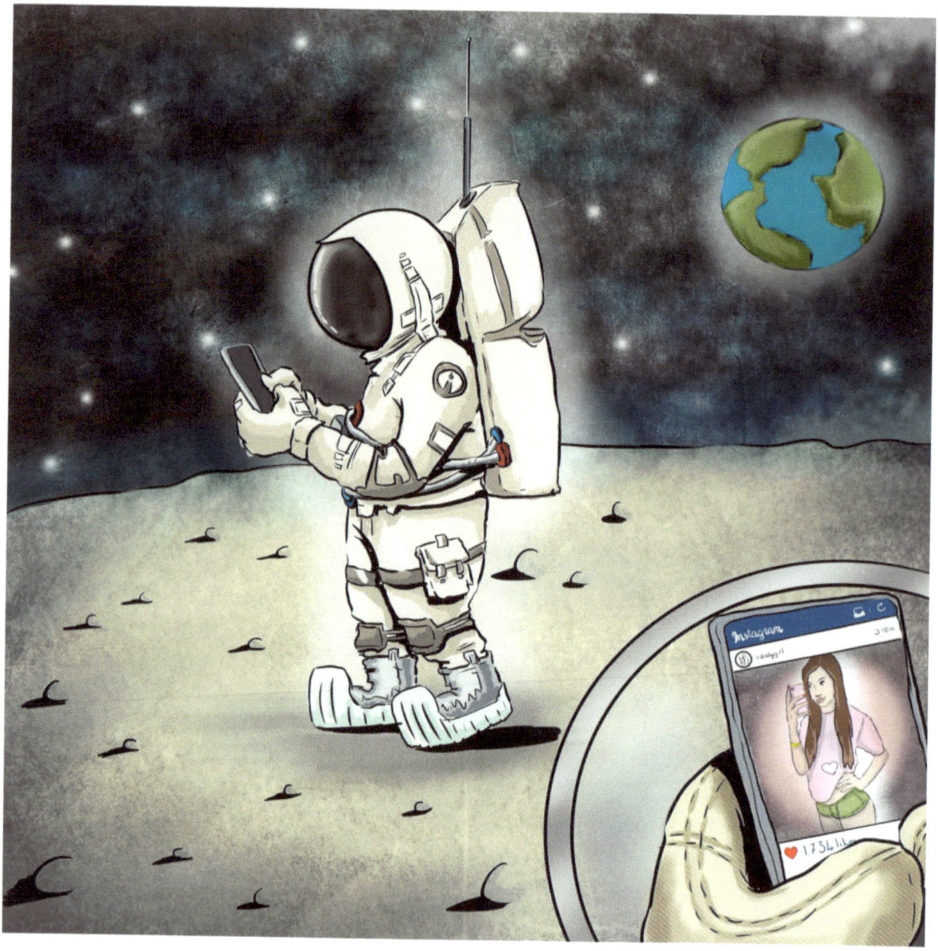
Instagram

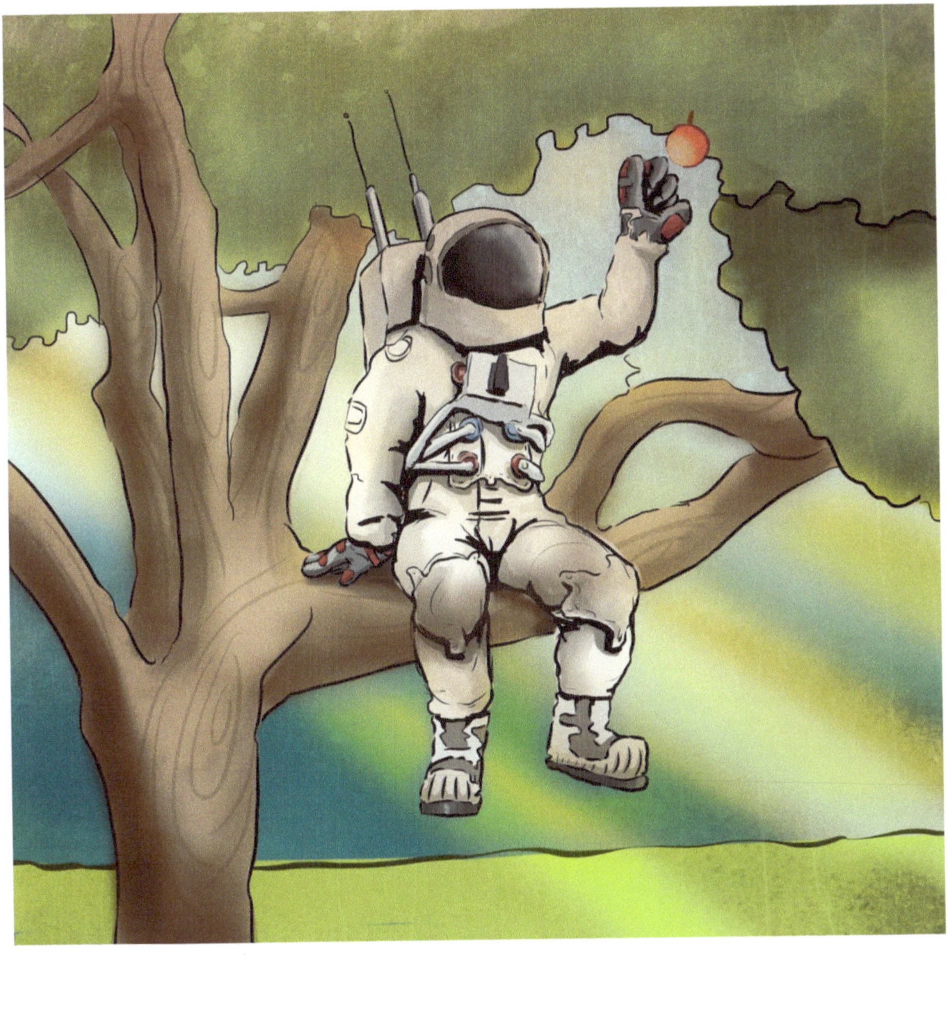

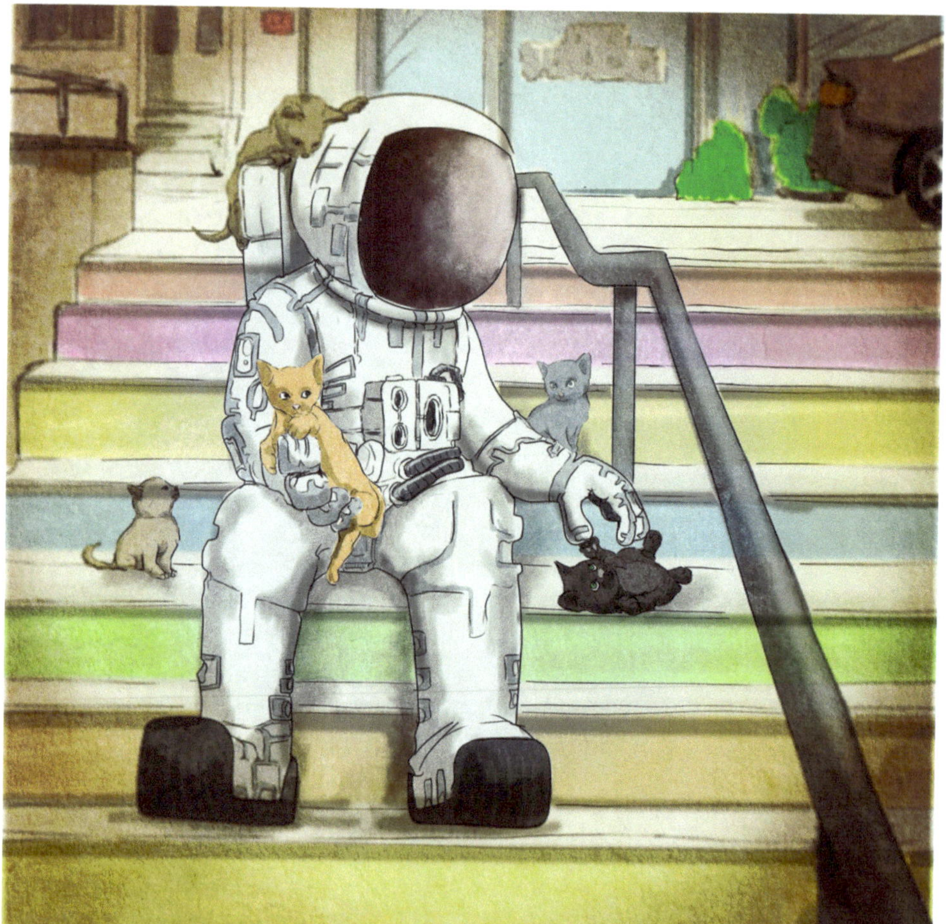

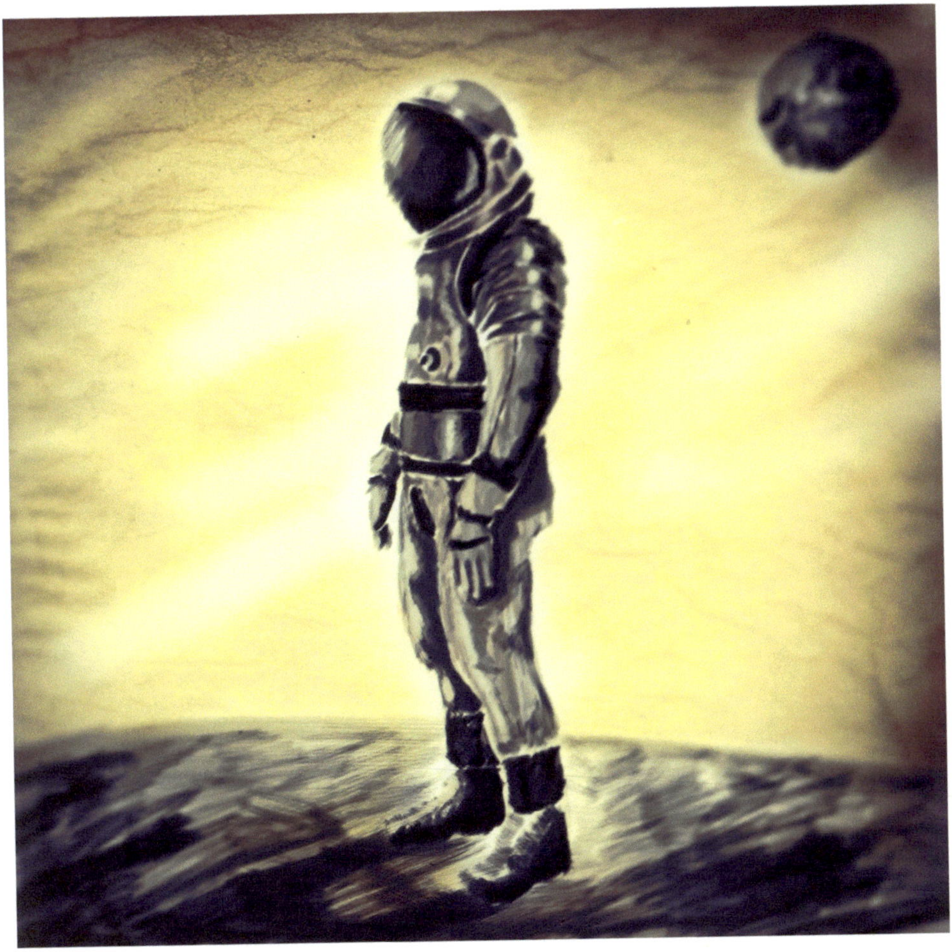

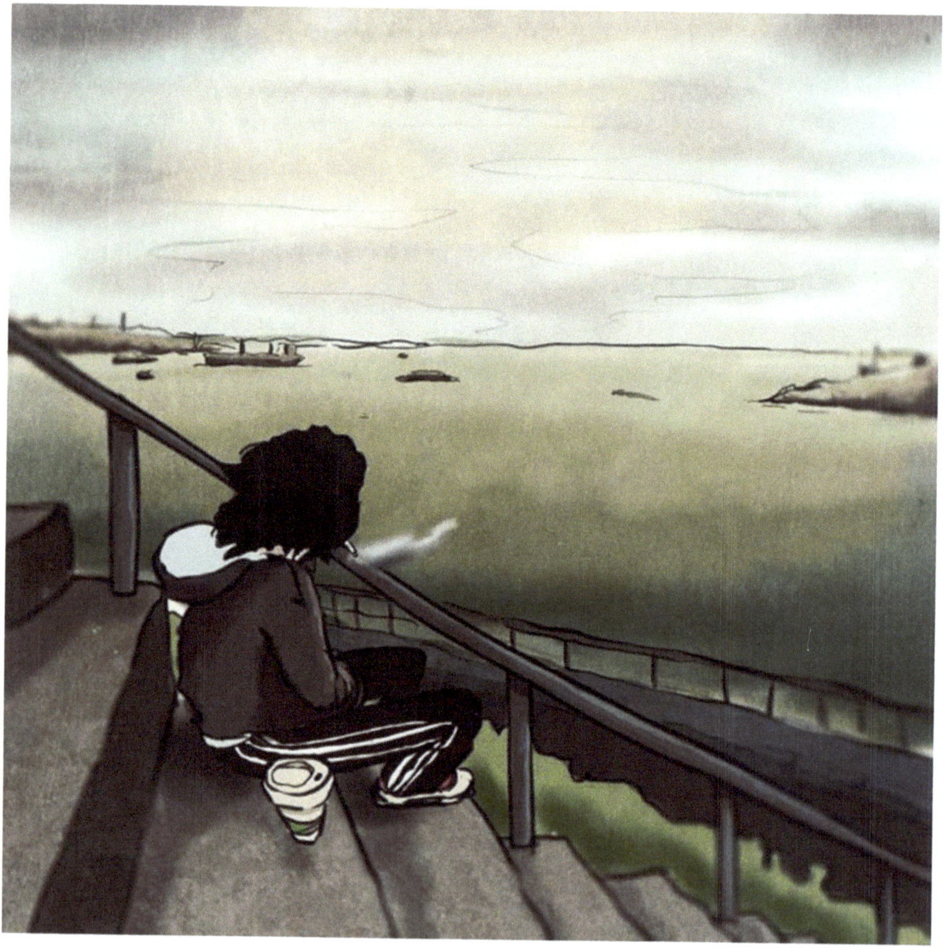

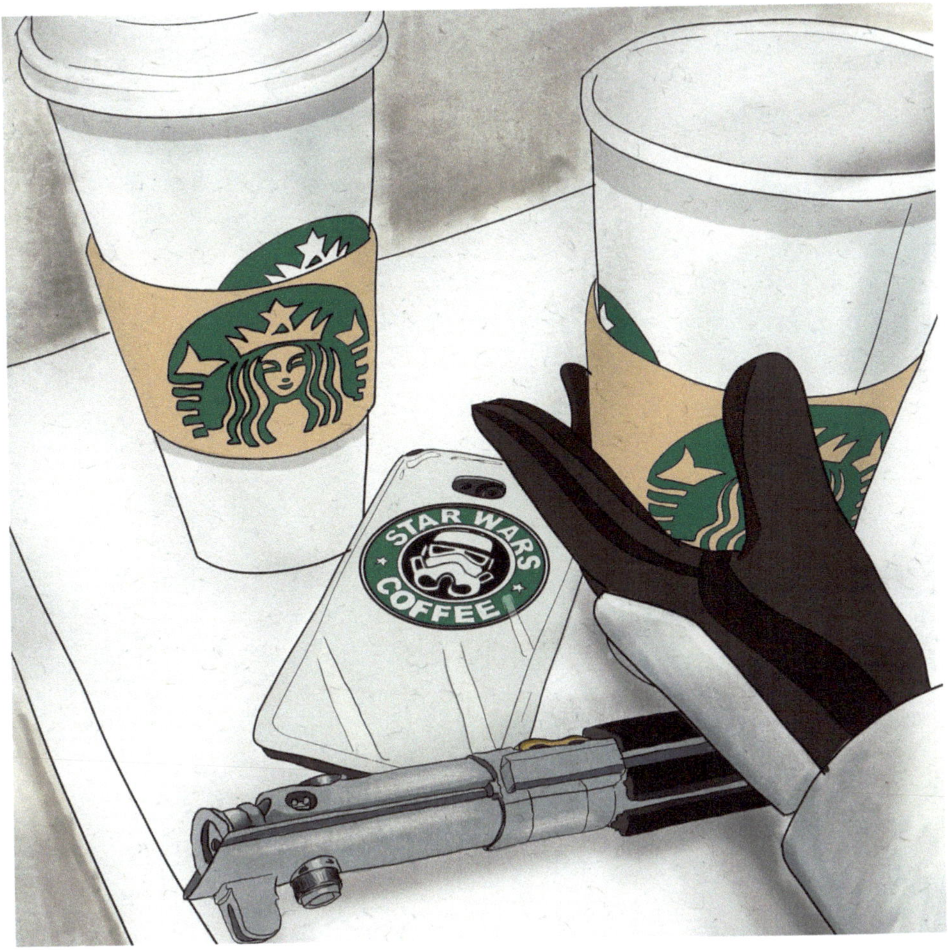
STAR WARS
COFFEE

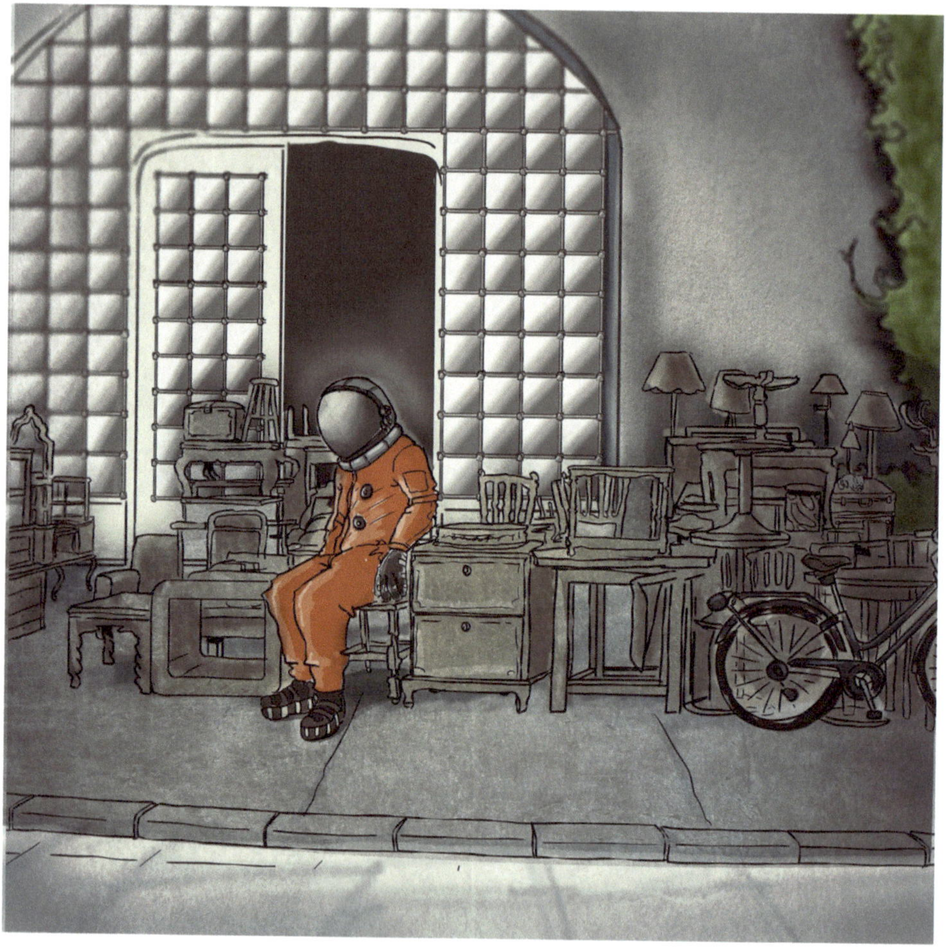

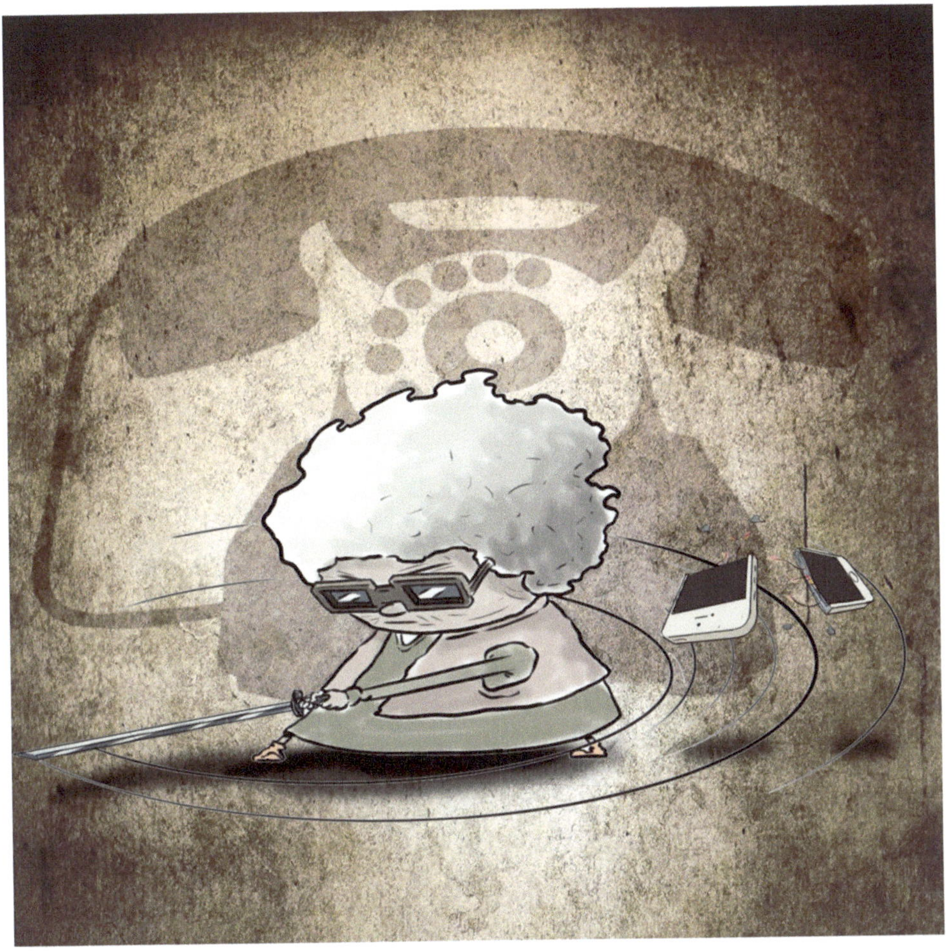

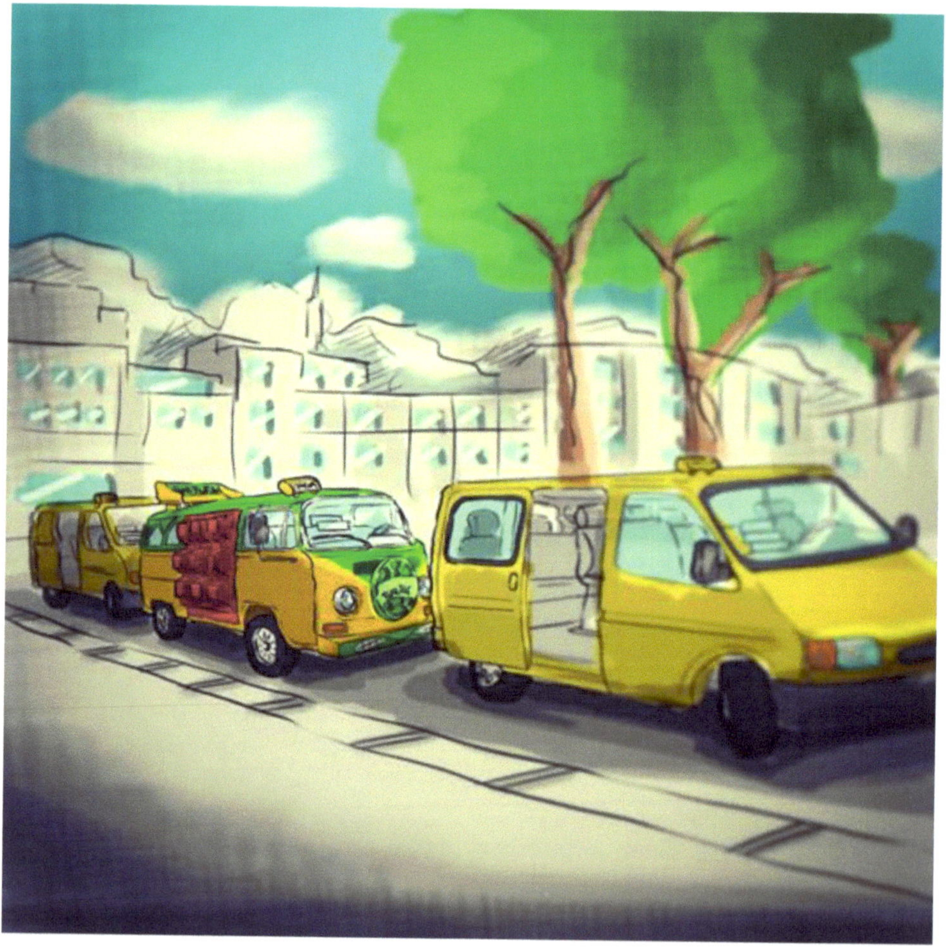

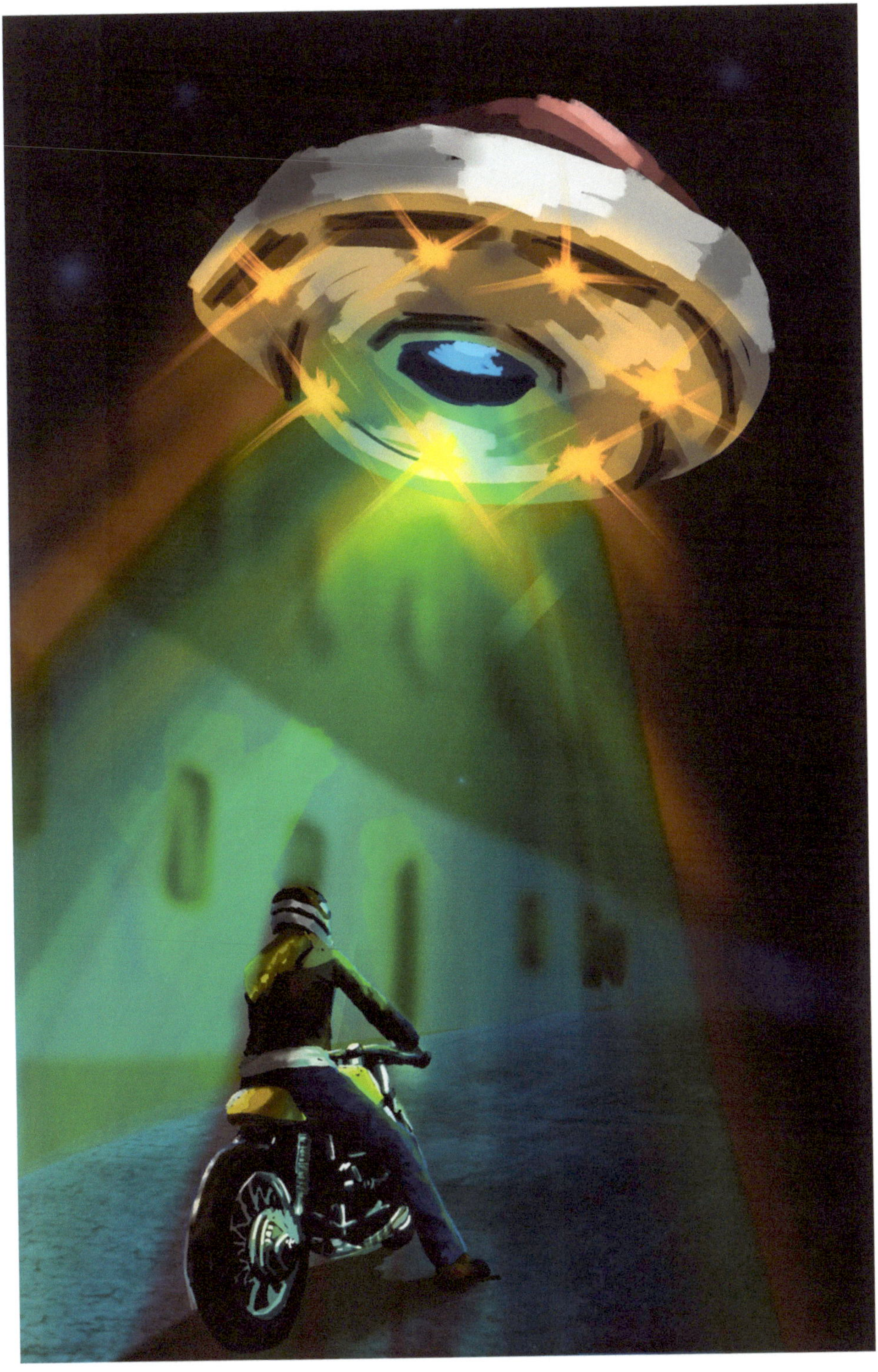

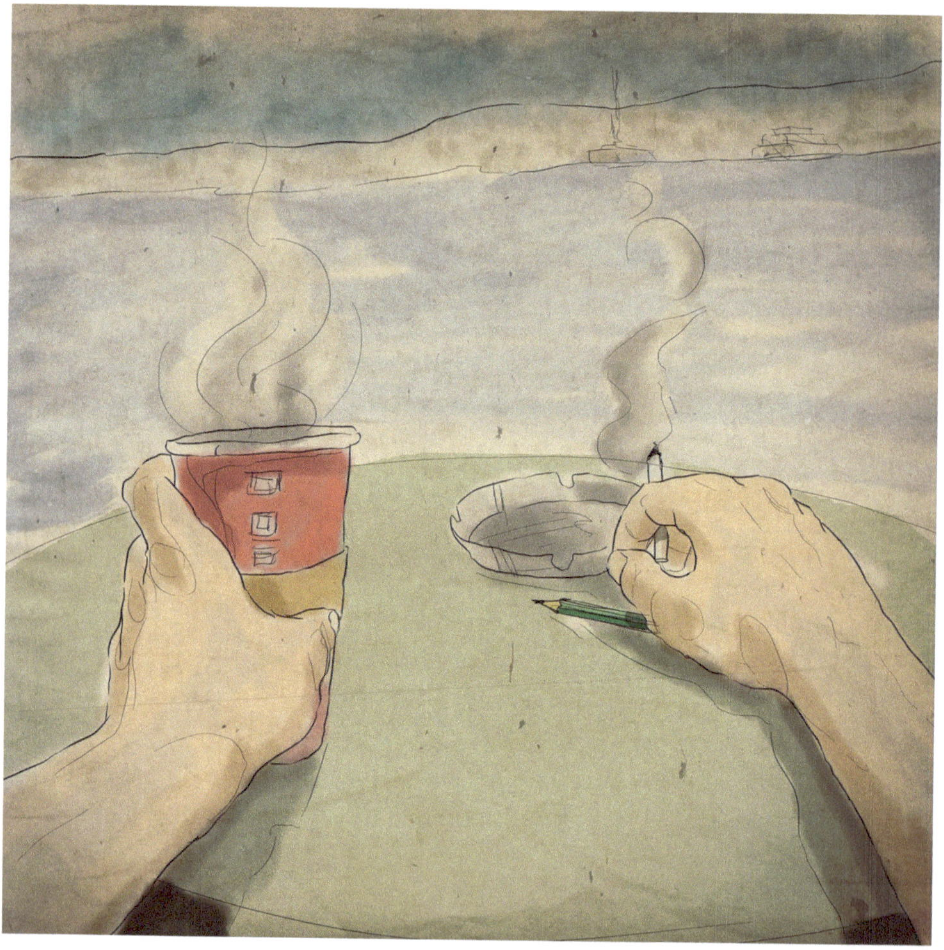

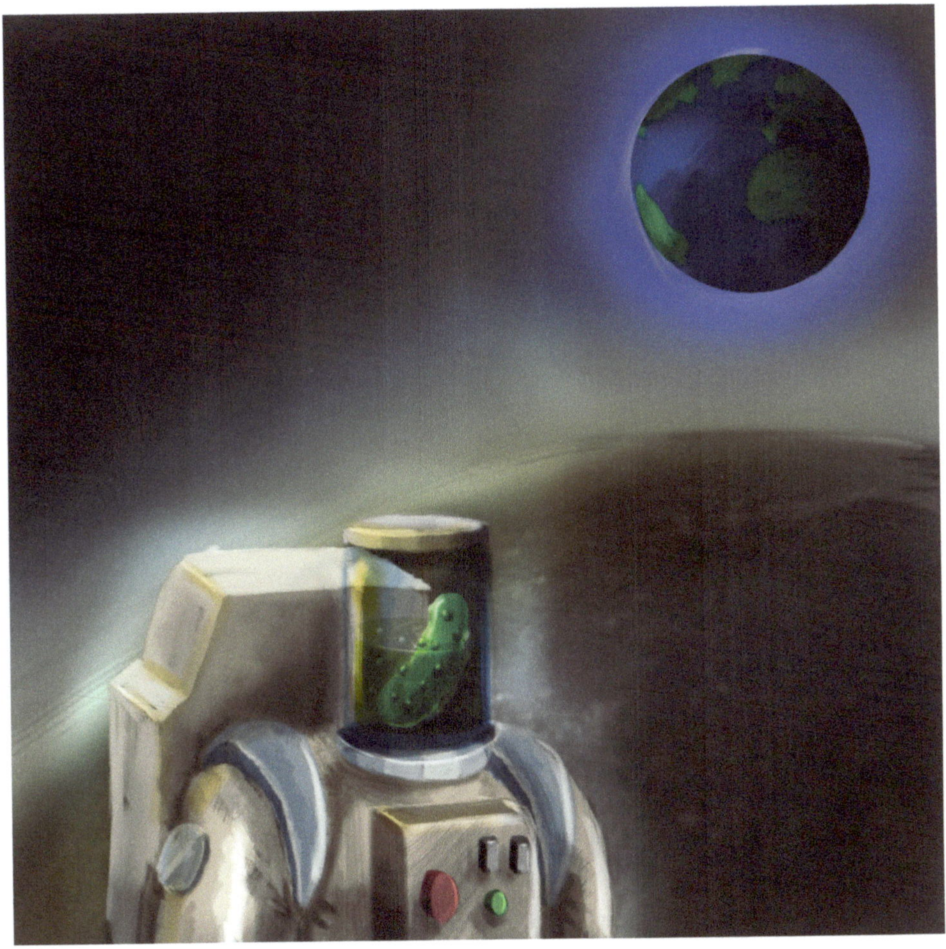

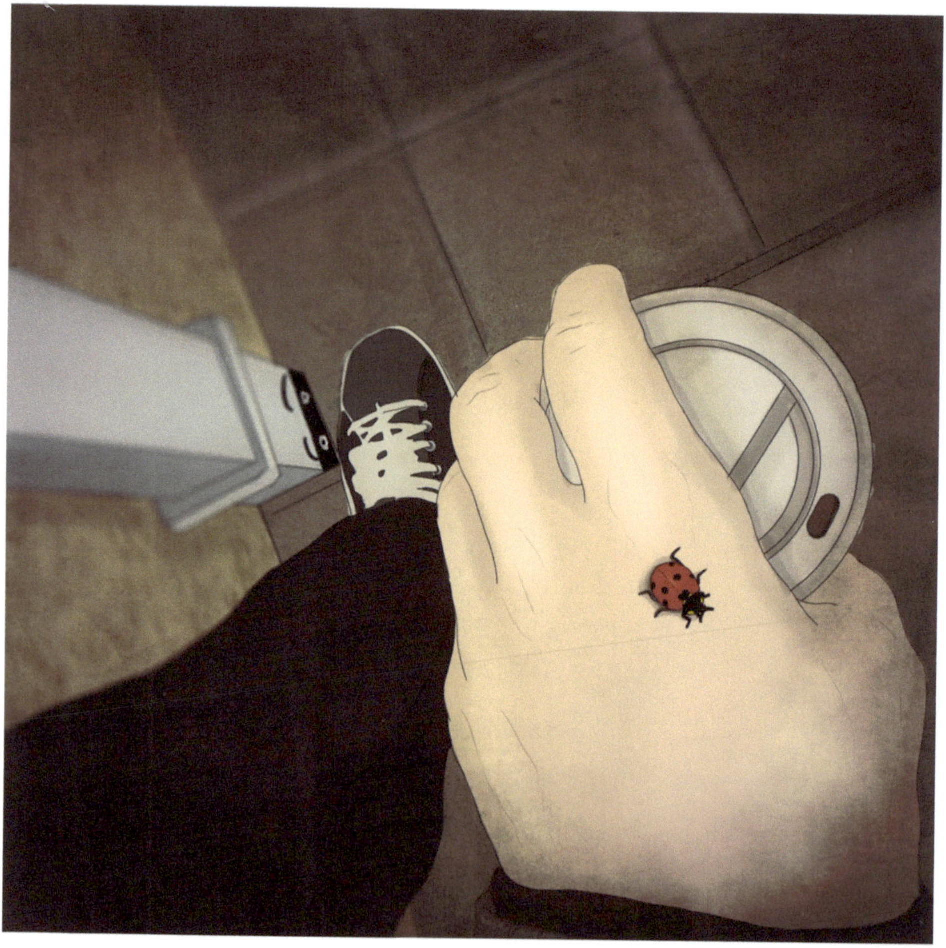

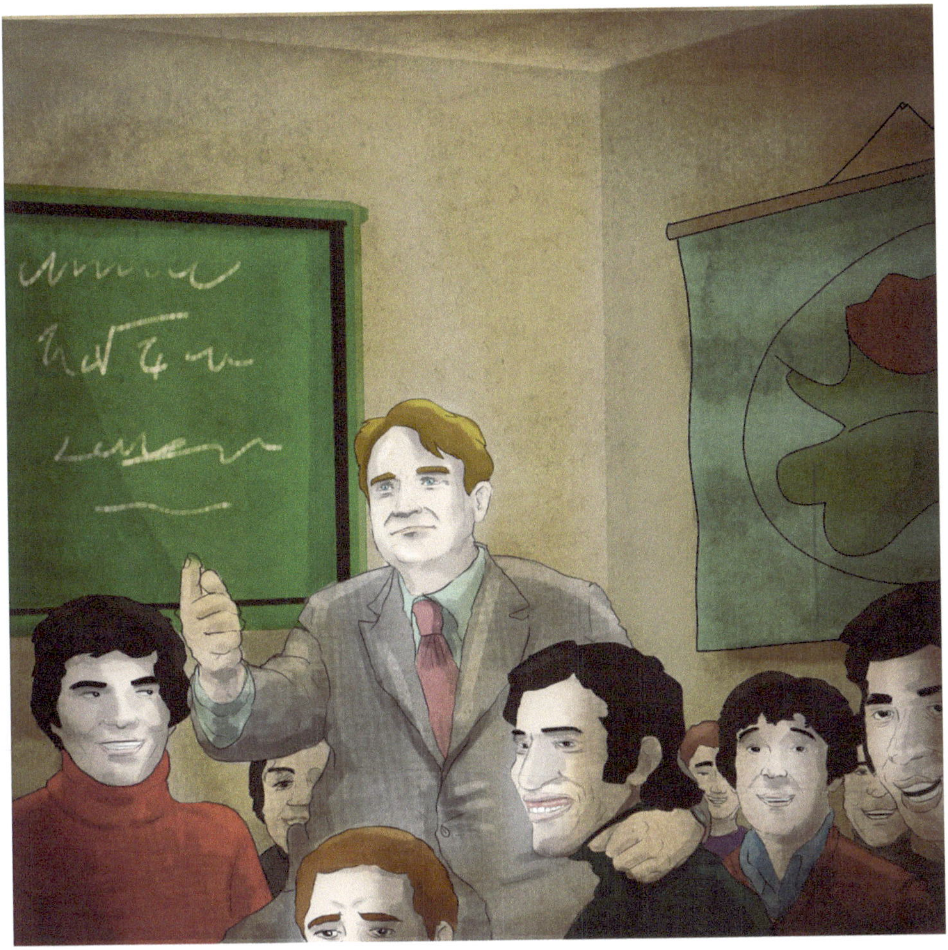

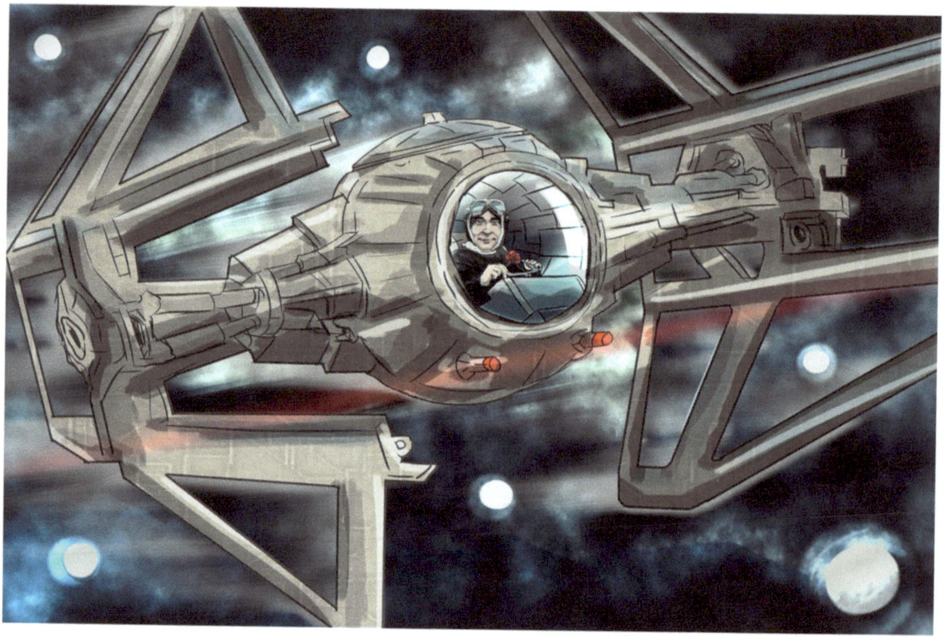

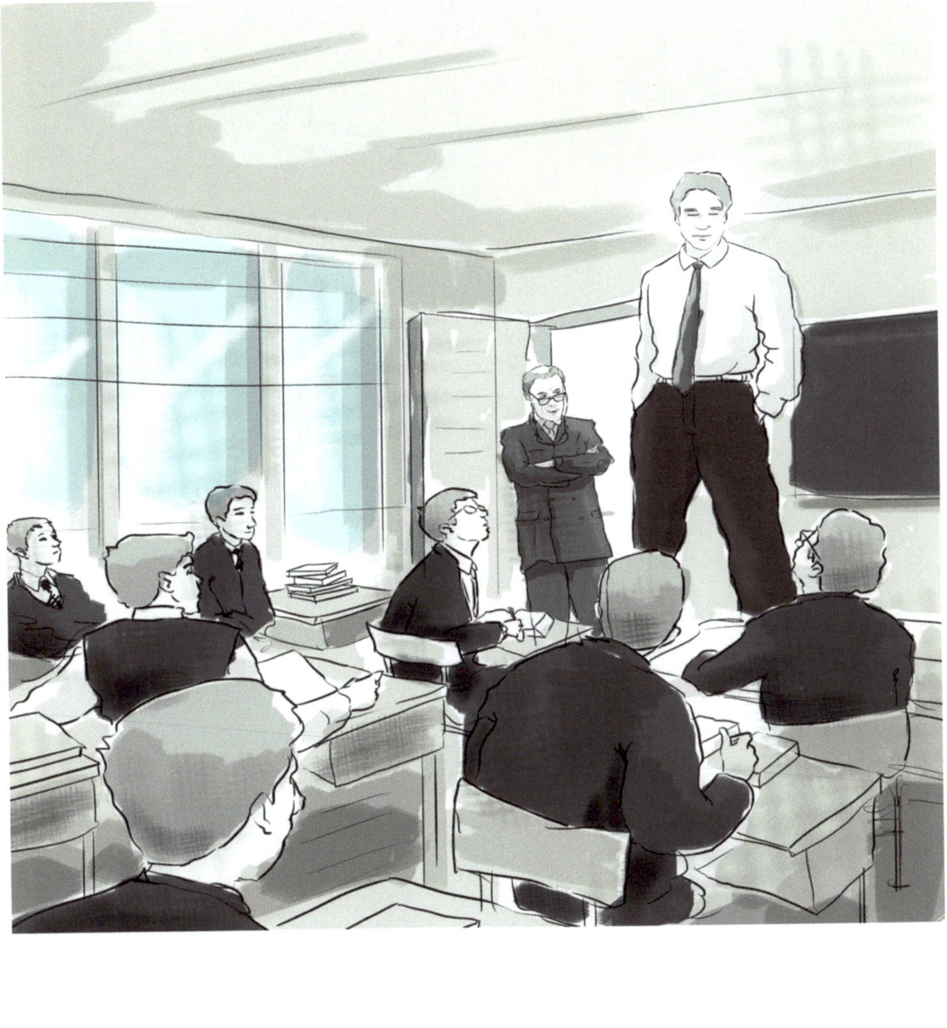

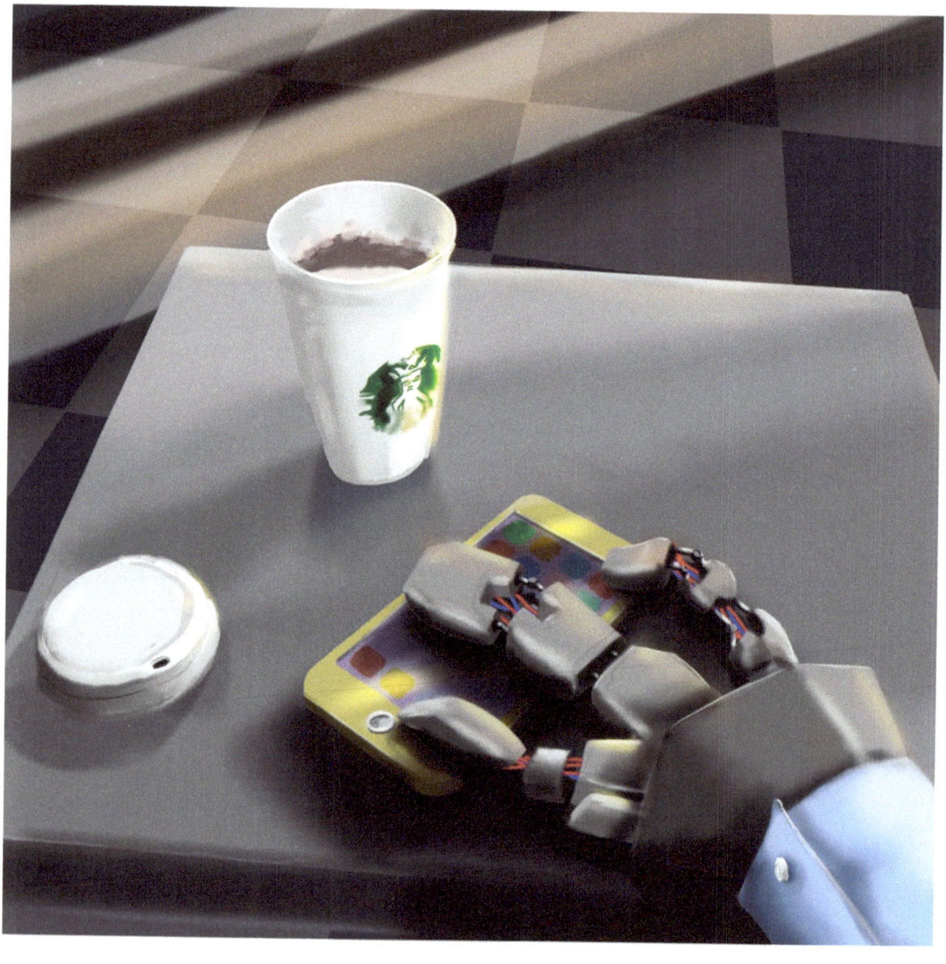

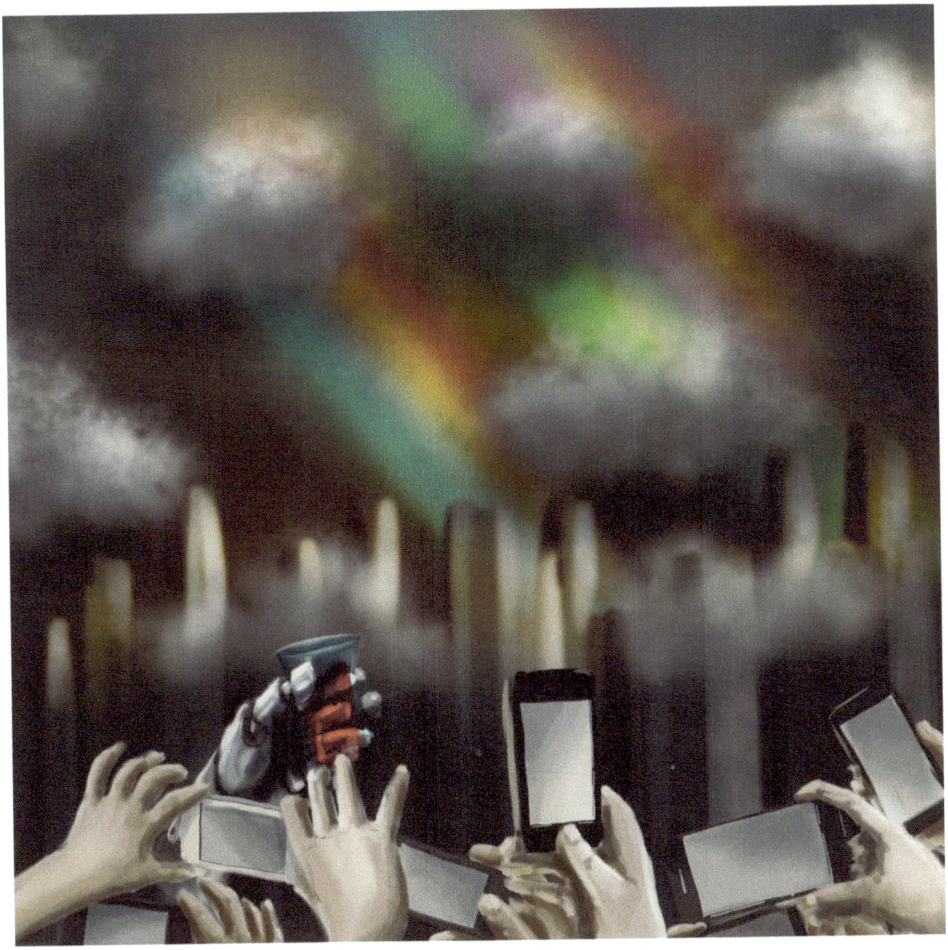

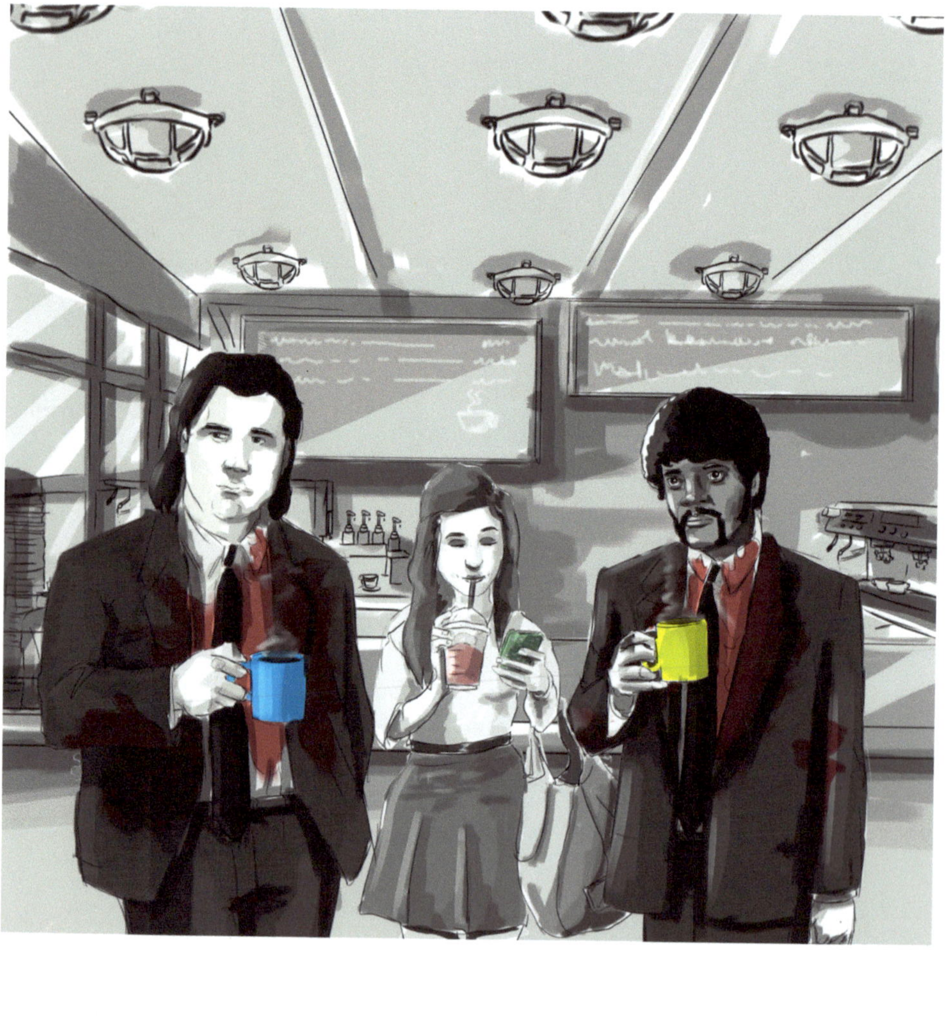

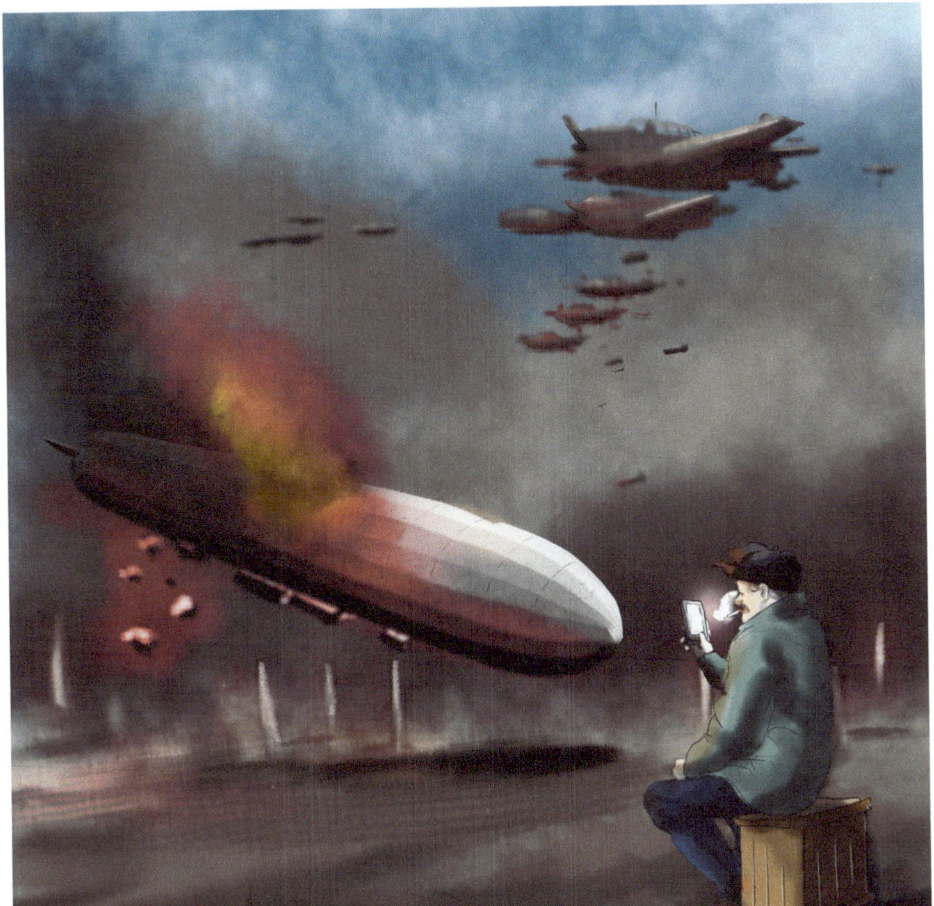

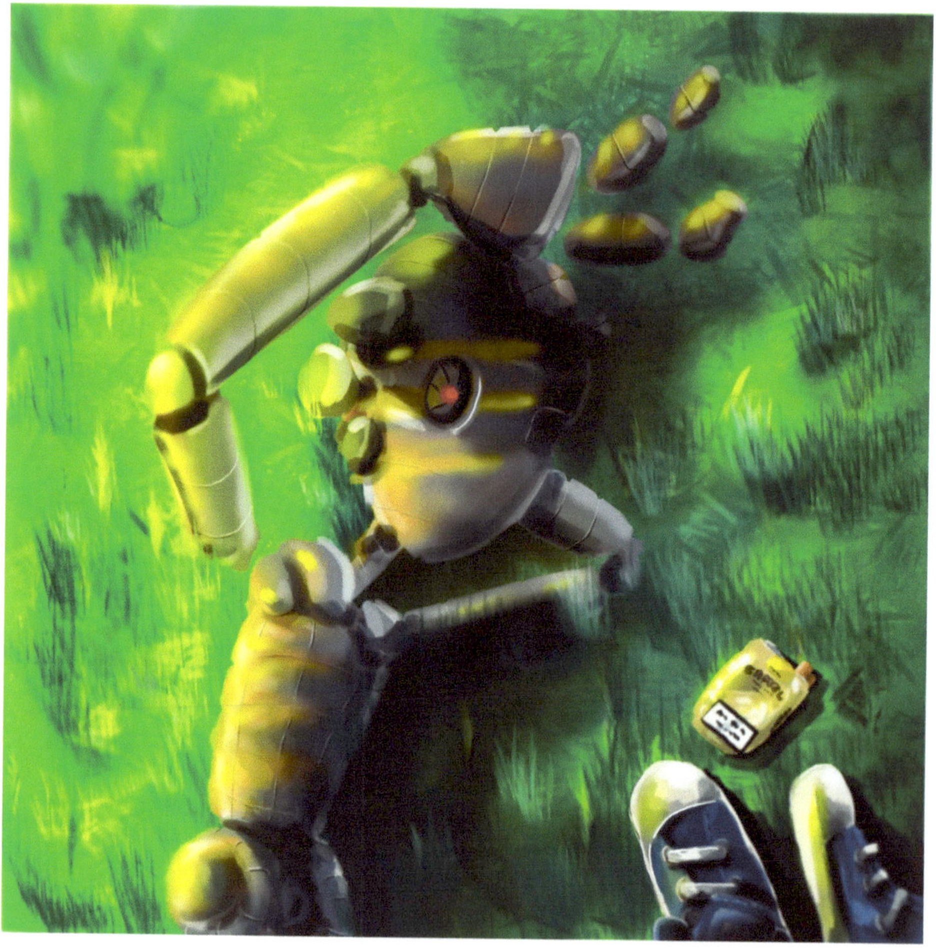

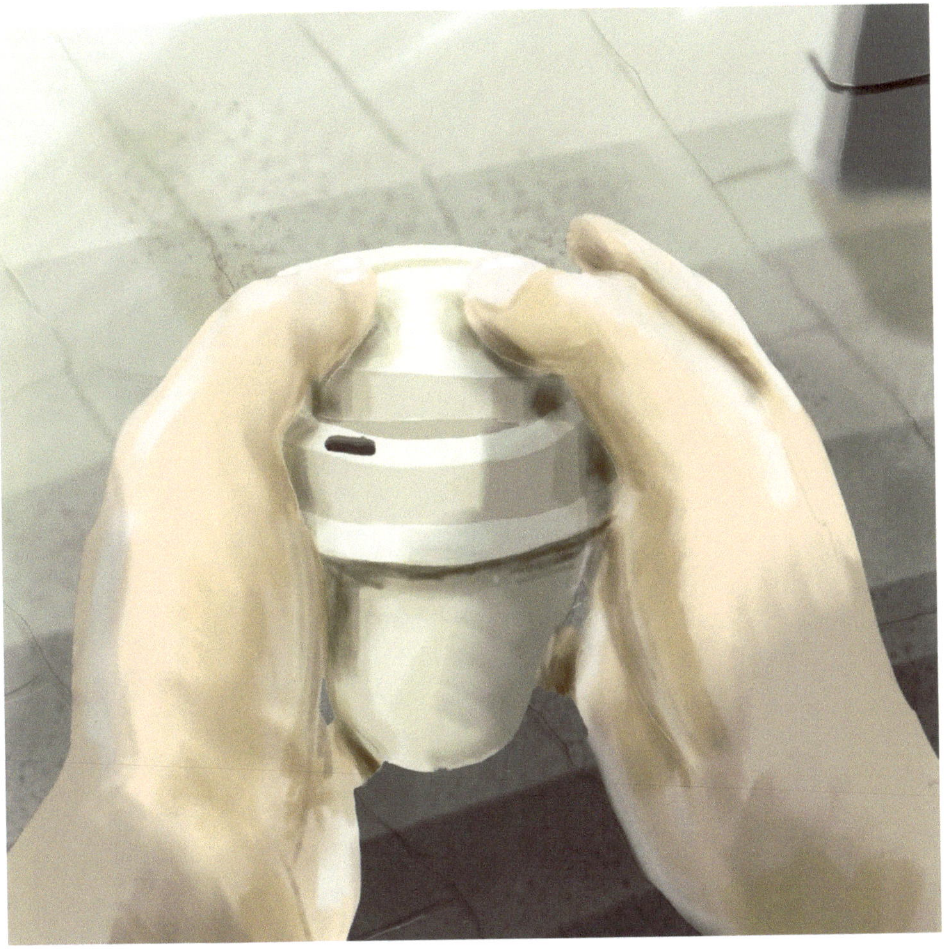

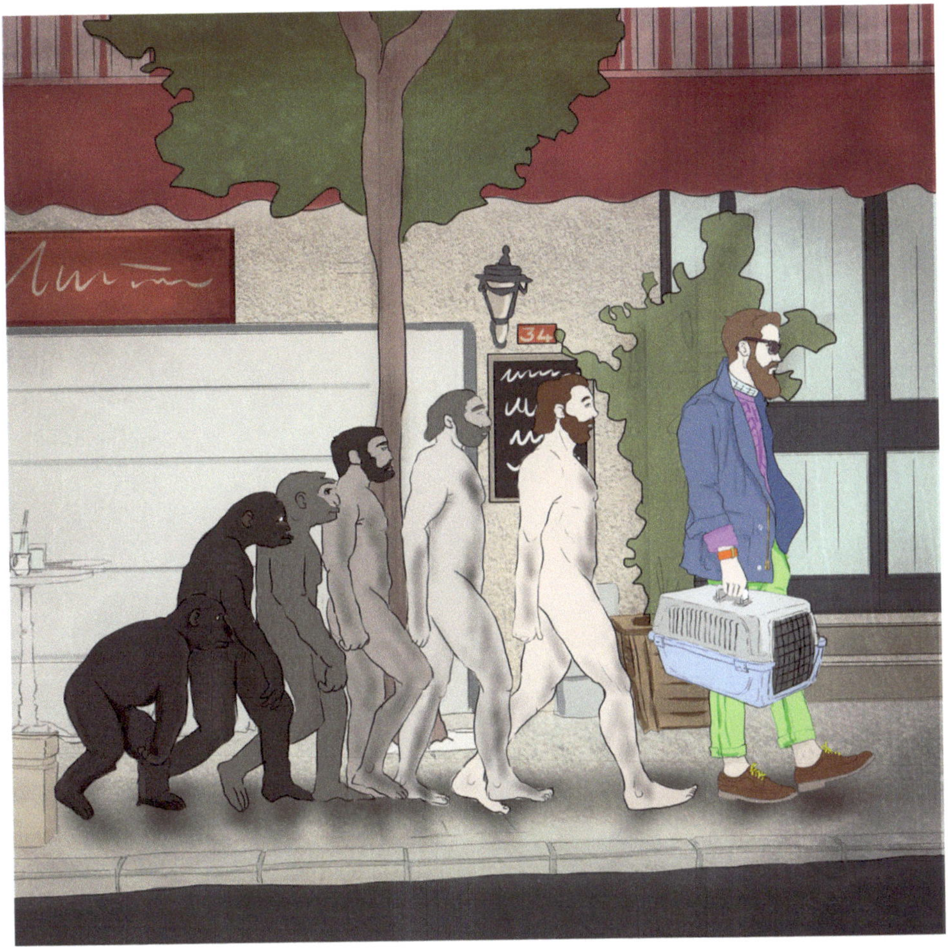
34

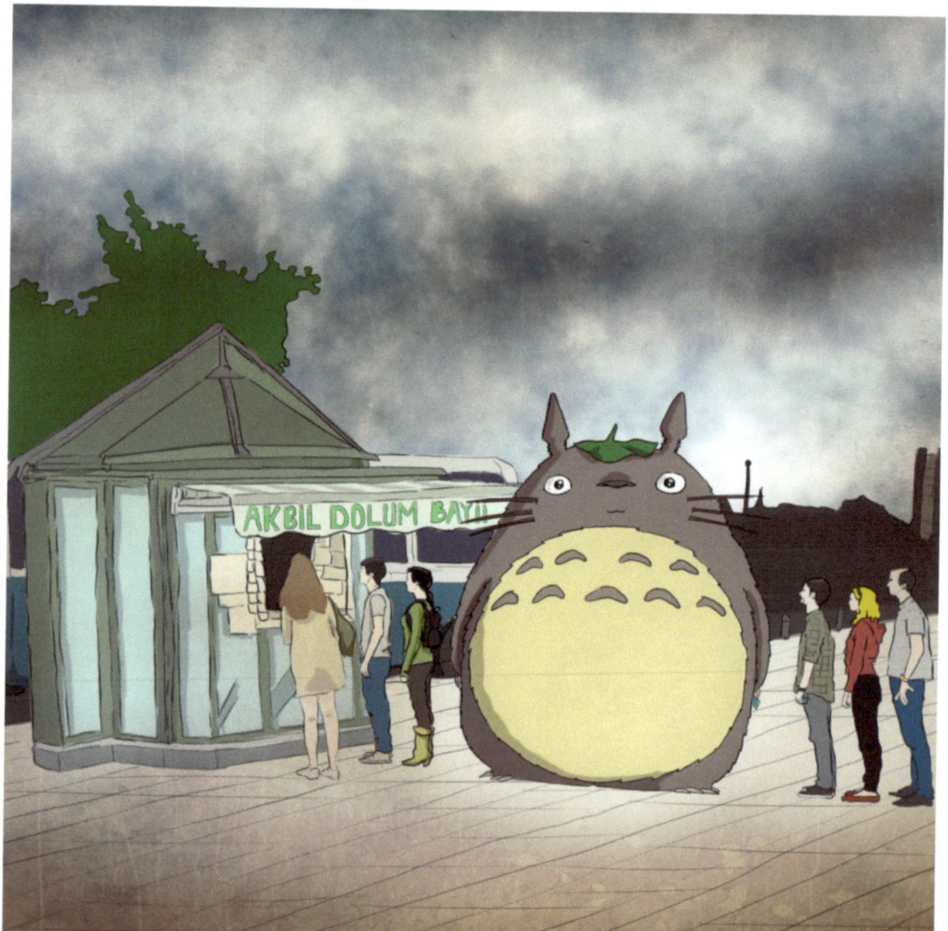
AKBIL DOLUM BAYII

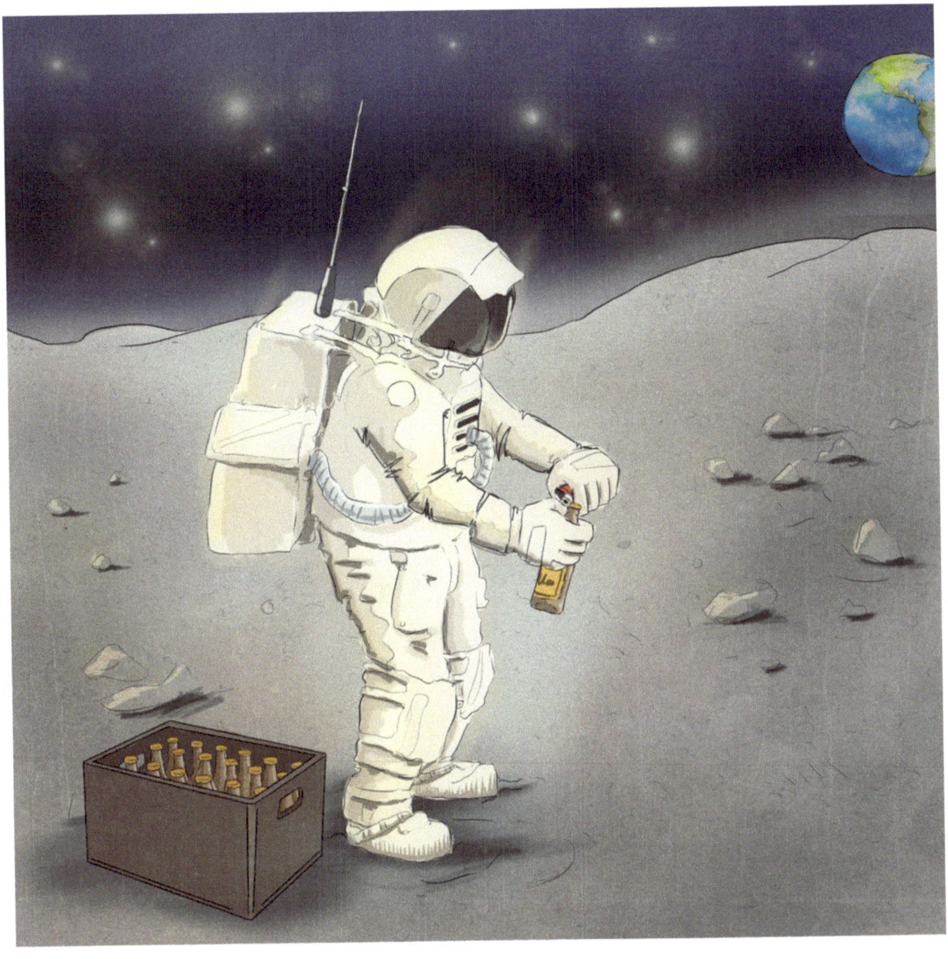

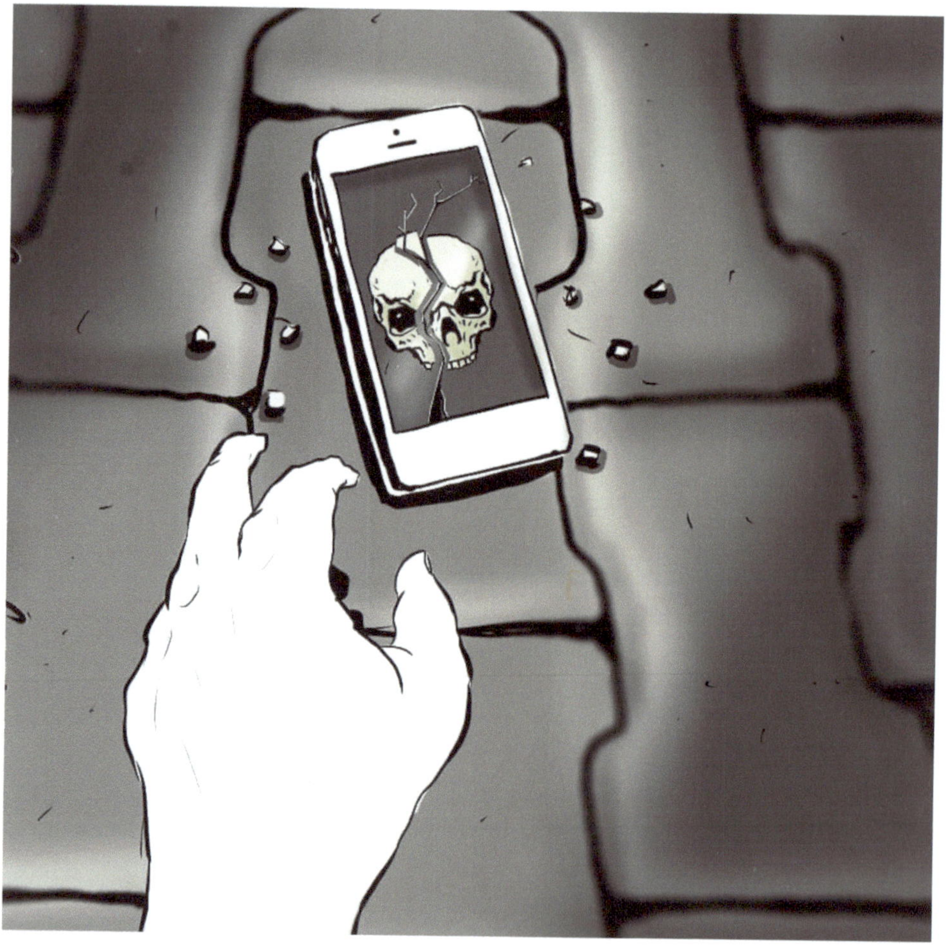

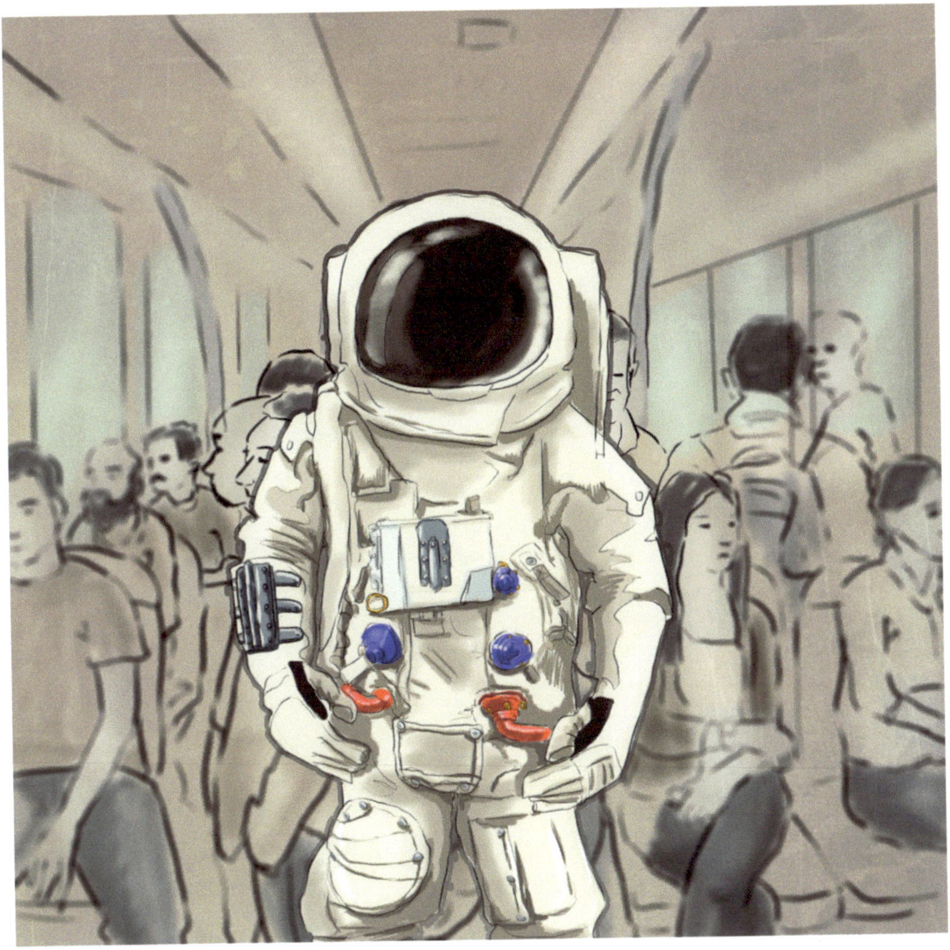

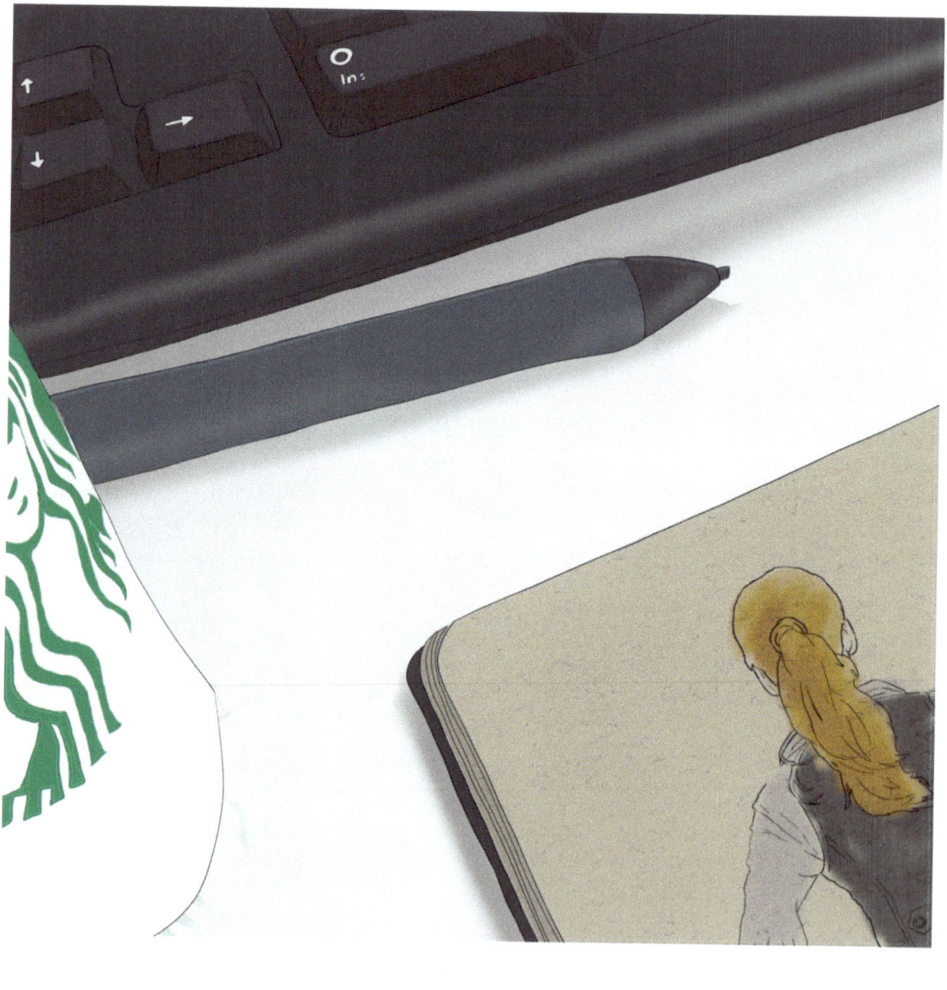
0
Ins

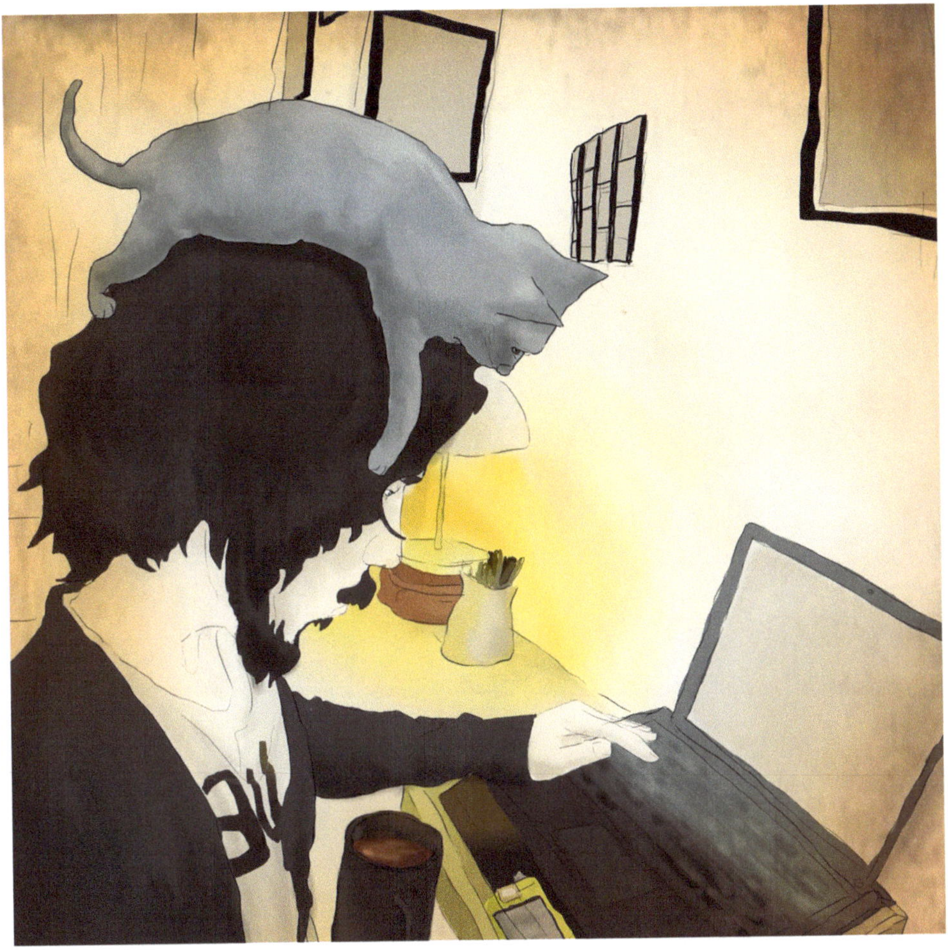

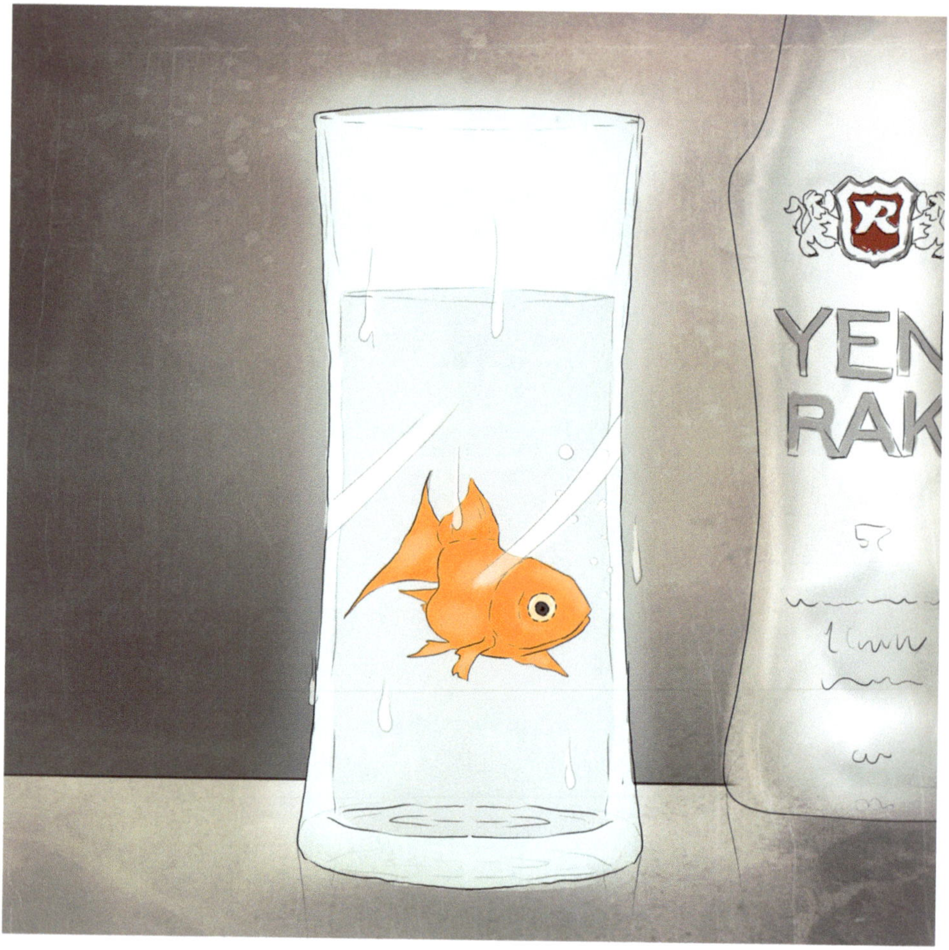
YEN
RAK

www.ingramcontent.com/pod-product-compliance
Lightning Source LLC
Chambersburg PA
CBHW040758240526
45474CB00008B/96
*9798335636711*